THE BOOK OF NATURE

By

Olaf Pedersen

University of Aarhus

SPECOLA VATICANA

1992

Vatican Observatory Publications

Distributed (except in Italy and Vatican City State) by:

THE UNIVERSITY OF NOTRE DAME PRESS
Notre Dame, Indiana 46556
USA

Distributed in Italy and Vatican City State by:

LIBRERIA EDITRICE VATICANA
V-00120 Città del Vaticano
Vatican City State

ISBN 0-268-00690-3

CONTENTS

FOREWORD

"THE MATTER IS URGENT"

In September 1987 at the Papal Summer Residence at Castel Gandolfo (Rome), which is also the headquarters of the Vatican Observatory, a Study Week was held on the topic: *Our Knowledge of God and Nature*. The official purpose for this event was the tricentennial commemoration of the publication of Isaac Newton's, *Philosophiae Naturalis Principia Mathematica*, the appearance of which might symbolically be regarded as the beginning of modern science. The intention was that the meeting should not be just a mere commemoration of this jubilee, but that it would make a serious contribution to the dialogue between science and theology. At the beginning of the book which resulted from that Study Week[1] there appeared an official letter of Pope John Paul II to "The Reverend George V. Coyne, S.J., Director of the Vatican Observatory", who was also one of the organizers of the meeting. In this letter the Pope wrote:

> The matter is urgent. Contemporary developments in science challenge theology far more deeply than did the introduction of Aristotle into Western Europe in the thirteenth century. Yet these developments also offer to theology a potentially important resource. Just as Aristotelian philosophy, through the ministry of such great scholars as St. Thomas Aquinas, ultimately came to shape some of the most profound expressions of theological doctrine, so can we not hope that the sciences of today, along with all forms of human knowing, may invigorate and inform those parts of the theological enterprise that bear on the relation of nature, humanity and God?[2]

The members of the faculty of the Center for Interdisciplinary Studies of the Academy of Theology in Cracow, in response to the original idea of Bishop Zycinski, who was then Dean of the Faculty of Philosophy of the Academy, have decided to organize each year a series of lectures which would develop topics treated in the Papal letter, especially those "that bear on the relation of nature, humanity and God", and they decided to reference them to the Papal letter by calling them the Coyne Lectures. The first in the series of the Coyne Lectures were delivered in October 1991 in Cracow by Professor Olaf Pedersen, an old friend of the Pontifical Academy of Cracow, whom I would now like to present.

v

Olaf Pedersen was born in 1920 at Egtved, Denmark. He studied at the Niels Bohr Institute in Copenhagen and in 1943 obtained his doctorate under C. Moller. From 1945 to 1950 he continued his studies with, among others, Etienne Gilson. In 1956 he began his career at the University of Aarhus as a lecturer in physics and in the history of science. In 1964 he joined the board of editors of *Centaurus*, a world famous journal devoted to the history of science. In 1965 he founded at the University of Aarhus the Institute of the History of Science, which very soon became known as a leading center in this branch of research.

Professor Pedersen is a member of many scientific societies. He was president of the *Académie Internationale d'Histoire des Sciences* and of the Commission 41 of the International Astronomical Union on the History of Astronomy and he was also vice-president of the International Union of the Philosophy of Science. He is also a visiting fellow of St. Edmund's College of the University of Cambridge, England. He has served on various international bodies, including: UNESCO, the Pastoral Council of Denmark, the Science and Theology Group of the Vatican Observatory, etc. In 1990 he retired from his position at the University of Aarhus.

His fields of research include: ancient and medieval astronomy, ancient mathematics, history of the calendar, science and theology, the works of Sacrobosco, Brahe, Galileo, Stensen, and Ørsted. Among his most significant publications are the books: *Early Physics and Astronomy, A Survey of the Almagest, Medieval Cosmology* and *Studium Generale*.

The three lectures, delivered by Professor Pedersen in Cracow and published here in this booklet, testify to his humble wisdom, whereby he is able to speak of the very distant past in such wise as to make the present more comprehensible. We hope that the tradition he has initiated in Cracow will continue to bear its fruit to the benefit of both science and theology.

Michael Heller

1.   *Physics, Philosophy and Theology: A Common Quest for Understanding*, eds. R.J. Russell, W.R. Stoeger, and G.V. Coyne (Notre Dame: University of Notre Dame Press, 1988).

2.   *Ibid.*, p. M12.

PREFACE

In 1990 the Pontifical Theological Academy of Cracow was kind enough to invite me to give the first series of the newly instituted Coyne Lectures. Since these lectures were named after a good friend who has, in recent years, contributed more than most other Catholic scientists to promote the debate on science and theology, I gratefully accepted this invitation, although I was fully aware that I would not be able to offer many new ideas or original thoughts. In fact, the lectures, which are here published in a somewhat expanded and revised version, have no other purpose than to provide some historical evidence for the view that the ongoing debate on science and religion is by no means exhausted by hackneyed references to the fate of Galileo or the quarrels following in the wake of the theory of evolution. For beneath both the ecclesiastical interventions of the past and the front-page sensationalism of the present there have existed all the time deep undercurrents of thought which testify to a profound harmony between the fundamental scientific belief in the rationality of the universe on the one hand, and the Christian belief in Christ as the eternal *logos* of the world on the other. Convinced that I share this perspective with the founders of the Pontifical Academy of Cracow, I dedicate to them the following much too brief, and perhaps also too selective, exposition of our common ideas.

Olaf Pedersen

I. THE BIRTH OF SCIENCE

The Great Metaphors

Over the ages the scientific description of nature has found it unavoidable to use a technical vocabulary of a more and more sophisticated character in order to gain precision and reduce ambiguity. But at the same time the general discourse on the universe has often been framed in terms of metaphors that have been able to absorb and express some of the fundamental attitudes of man towards the world. Such metaphors can be nothing more than pictures which seem to present a part or the whole of the universe in analogy with something with which man has become familiar in his own world. As pictures they exist only in the eye of the beholder. Consequently, they are always open to more than one interpretation. But far from being a defect this essential openness is the reason why a number of these metaphors have had a very long life and have been able to survive great changes both in science and in the social background against which they first appeared. A few examples will illustrate such an ability to survive and will explain why the study of metaphors is a fascinating element of the history of science, from which much insight can be gained.

In the Middle Ages it was customary to speak of the "Sun as King" of the universe. Behind this metaphor was a cosmology (inherited from Greek antiquity) in which the sun was supposed to circle around the earth in the middle of the planets[1] so that Venus, Mercury and the Moon were between the sun and the earth, and Mars, Jupiter and Saturn between the sun and the firmament of the fixed stars which formed the outer boundary of the world. The six other planets were the "subjects" of the king who could be said to "govern" them, since the motion of the sun clearly influenced the motions of the planets as observed from the earth. This was reflected in the theories of Ptolemy in which the annual motion of the sun entered as a component into each of the different kinematical mechanisms by which the positions of the planets were determined. Consequently, it would seem that the metaphor of the "Sun as King" was intimately connected with the old geocentric system of the world.[2]

Against this background it seems rather difficult to understand why Copernicus was also able to call the sun the king of the universe.[3] Now the sun was at rest at the center of the world, its apparent motion explained by the motion of the earth, and its "governance" of the planets explained away as a reflection of the latter. How could the metaphor survive such a drastic change of cosmology? The answer is that the idea of kingship had also changed. In the Middle Ages the king lived on horse-back, travelling around his realm to keep a watchful eye on his rebellious barons. But now the king had become the head of a more centralized government, ruling his country from a capital where he could stay at rest and from where the rays of his power and glory would penetrate the surrounding territory. This must be the reason why the metaphor was able to stay alive despite both an astronomical and a political revolution. It had no fixed significance, but only a poetic force that was strong enough to withstand the vicissitudes of the changing circumstances.

An equally famous and even more long-lived metaphor was the "World as a Clock". Trying to refute the assumptions of the atomists in antiquity Cicero said that

> . . . when you look at a sundial or a water-clock you infer that it tells the time by art and not by chance. How can it then be inconsistent to suppose that the universe, which includes both the works of art in question, the craftsmen who made them, and everything else, can be devoid of purpose and reason? [4]

Behind this argument was a feeling of awe in face of the majestic order and regularity of the heavenly motions which Cicero in the same connection compared to the "orrery" (*sphaera*) "recently constructed by our friend Posidonius". Two thousand years later the metaphor was still alive. The deistic philosophers of the Enlightenment delighted in the idea of the world as a mechanical clock which the Great Clockmaker (called The Deity) had wound once and for all before leaving it to perform its regular course without further intervention. Thus the metaphor now served to affirm God as Creator at the same time as it denied the divine providence by which the creation is upheld. Later on we shall see still another use of the same metaphor by 18th century Christian theologians, for whom the intricate mechanism of the pocket watch was a picture of the complexity of the universe and a testimony to the intelligence of its author.

With this expression we are already approaching the third and last of the three great metaphors to which I wish to draw attention. The "Book of Nature" was in several ways the most fertile and provocative among the symbolic pictures of the world. It immediately raised a number of questions. If nature is a "book" we must ask first of all in which language it is written? Can it be decoded? Can we be sure that it contains a meaning or conveys a message? What does it tell us? And by whom was it written? Over the ages these and many similar questions have been asked again and again, and the answers have formed a running commentary on the changing preoccupations of natural philosophy. In particular, the idea of nature as some kind of book points to the intimate connection between science as a quest for insight into the operations of nature on the one hand and, on the other, the language in which such insight can be expressed and communicated. This is one of the reasons why this particular metaphor has been able to serve more different purposes than any other.

But there is also another reason that explains why the metaphor of the Book of Nature became especially prominent in the Christian world, from its first appearance here and there in the writings of the Fathers of the Church, until it was on almost every lip of both lay and learned in the century of the Enlightenment and even thereafter. For in the Christian tradition there was also another book, and that a real one, from which insight could be obtained. The Holy Scriptures of the Bible were universally acclaimed as the unique testimony of God's self-disclosure as creator and redeemer of the world. This established a dialectical relationship between the two books, with more questions to be explored and answered. Were the two books equally authentic and reliable? Did they treat of the same subject matter? Would the reading of the one contribute to a better understanding of the other? What would happen if they were found to contradict one another? Problems like these explain why the interaction between natural science and Christian faith was so often shaped in the form of a discourse on the two great books, and also why the study of this interaction could do worse than follow the historical development of the idea of the Book of Nature, even if this title was given to the world several centuries after the fundamental idea had emerged. Since science is considerably older than Christianity we shall begin our investigation at a very early stage of history.

The Mythological Discourse on Nature

In all known civilizations there was a time when the Book of Nature was a book of stories told in the ordinary language of everyday human life. Consequently, all events in both nature and society were seen as the results of the free decisions of a variety of personal agents, men and women acting in the human world, and a multitude of gods and spirits operating through the phenomena of nature. Everything formed an interlocking whole without any sharp distinction between the natural and the moral universe.[5] Remember the story of the shipwreck of Odysseus. This catastrophe came about because his hungry crew stole and ate the sacred oxen of Thrikinia. This had repercussions in the upper world, since the oxen were guarded by the long-skirted Lampetia who was the daughter of Helios, the sun-god, and she reported the incident to her father. Helios alerted Zeus in whose power it was to send the storm and the lightning that destroyed the ship.[6] So nature was personalistic through and through just like society. Even as rare and transient a phenomenon as the rainbow was personified as the Lady Iris who acted as the messenger of the gods.[7] No wonder that the mythological stories about nature were described as "theology" when this word made its first entrance into world literature.[8]

The mythological discourse on nature had several important corollaries. The gods of nature were freely acting agents. Mortal beings could never know what they had in mind for the future. Consequently, the arts of divination flourished all over the ancient world in many different forms. The flight of birds, or the liver of a sacrificial sheep might be portents of coming events. Dreams and oracles might be interpreted as divine messages. Most of this is now forgotten; but we are still confronted with the long-lived belief in astrology which originated at least four thousand years ago in ancient Mesopotamia. Here the most powerful gods were identified with the Sun, the Moon and the five planets that are visible to the naked eye. It followed that the mutual "aspects" of these stars, i.e. their conjunctions, oppositions, quadratures, etc., as well as their positions relative to the 12 constellations of the zodiac, might reveal the future course of events if they were duly interpreted by expert astrologers (who in Mesopotamia were officially employed by the king). Since the motions of the planets were found to be periodical the idea emerged that all events in both nature and society would repeat themselves with a regular period that was sometimes called the "Great Year".

Having looked over the shoulders of the gods, man might try to influence their decisions. Here two essentially different ways were open. If the freedom of the gods was respected they might be persuaded by prayers, gifts, or sacrifices in the same way as free human beings. This was the religious way, but it might also be tempting to try to force the will of the gods by magical procedures which they would be unable to resist. From this point of view religion and magic are clearly distinct responses, although it must be admitted that their line of demarcation can be difficult to trace. The priest and the sorcerer often operated on the same terrain, and many old texts reveal the fact that a magical incantation may also give expression to an authentically religious attitude.

Before the mythological discourse on nature is condescendingly discarded as "primitive" and "unscientific" it might be worth-while to reflect briefly upon its advantages. First and foremost it was simple in the sense that it was expressed in a language derived from daily human affairs. Therefore, even children could understand it. Moreover, the ways of nature were lucid in so far as its gods acted on the same principles as human beings, being motivated by similar reasons or passions. Consequently, the myths of the gods could be told in a way that made room for much human wisdom. Finally, the mythological account was all-embracing, since both the mortals and the gods were united in one single "society". Therefore, there was no gap between nature and culture, just as the distinction between "science" and "religion" did not occur.

The Birthpangs of Science

Whereas the mythological discourse made man familiar with nature it had also less satisfactory characteristics. It gave no unified account of the phenomena which were explained *ad hoc*, and sometimes by a variety of mutually contradictory stories. For instance, the ancient Egyptians had at least four more or less incompatible cosmological myths about the origin of the world, although with a noticeable stress on the importance of water as a common feature. Moreover, by referring the phenomena to the free decisions of the gods, the old discourse was unable to account for the obvious regularities in nature. Hesiod explained the low altitude of the sun in winter time by saying that Helios had travelled to the south in order to shine over the land of the Ethiopians.[9] But, if winter comes because the sun-god has decided to go away, how could one be sure that he would return at the right time of the year for the harvest to be gathered so that society could survive? The annual rites of the mystery religions tried to safeguard the proper succession of the seasons by religious and magical means. But were such rites really necessary? Would not spring follow upon winter also in years when the ceremonies were badly performed or perhaps even omitted?

We have no single text which documents conscious reflections along such lines. But we know that there came a time when the old idea of nature as the playground of the gods began to flounder. This happened in the Greek world around the sixth century B.C., that is, at a time marked by great intellectual and moral commotion all over the world. The Buddha in India, Lao Tse and Confucius in China, and the great prophets of Israel were more or less the contemporaries of the first Greek philosophers in the Ionian colonies on the coast of Asia Minor, who launched the truly new idea that the phenomena of nature were not caused by arbitrary decisions of personal deities. On the contrary, any phenomenon was now supposed to emerge as a consequence of an immanent and impersonal necessity which forced it to appear any time the right conditions were at hand. Why this idea first came to light among the Greeks, and how it may have been related to the intellectual development in the countries to the East of the Greek world are historical questions which we need not consider here. Instead we shall reflect briefly upon the purely linguistic difficulties with which the first pioneers of the new conception of nature had to wrestle.

Central to this conception was the idea that the various phenomena are produced by an inescapable "necessity" that links them together in chains of "cause" and "effect". The problem was that the already established Greek language had no particular words for such abstract concepts. This prevented the first natural philosophers from saying clearly and without ambiguity what they wished to express. Consequently, the new, non-mythological discourse on nature could not emerge full-fledged from the genius of a single mind. It had to grope its way through a linguistic crisis, simply because ordinary language was not prepared to cope with it. This seems to be the lot of any radically new insight which contradicts the wisdom of the past, and is, therefore, homeless in the language of the past, unless the past is reformed or enriched with a new and suitable vocabulary. The extant fragments of the pre-Socratic philosophers shed a flickering light on how the Greeks tried to overcome this crisis in two essentially different ways.

A beautiful illustration of the first way is found in Herodotus who worked out a non-mythological theory of the inundation of the Nile, which he ascribed to the annual motion of the sun, saying that the sun was the *aitia* of this enigmatic phenomenon.[10] This was a strange choice of words for in ordinary Greek *aitia* meant the guilt of a criminal who had offended against the law; so literally speaking Herodotus branded the sun as a criminal, and even an habitual criminal, since it acts in the same way year after year. And when we remember that an inundation is no crime at all, but a blessing for all the land of the Egyptians, we must admit that this attempt to establish non-personal links in nature led to a breakdown of ordinary language. Nevertheless, philosophers continued to say *aitia* until the word acquired by force of habit that sense of "cause" with which we are now familiar.

Similar developments took place with other key words. For instance, the fundamental concept of "necessity" was expressed by the word *ananke*, which literally meant the various means, from persuasion to torture, by which a criminal was made to confess.[11] In this way the linguistic crisis seemed to be overcome within the domain of everyday language. This no doubt made it easier for the new concept of nature to develop and spread. Nevertheless, this solution was illusory, since it consisted in a metaphorical use of everyday words which were deprived of their original meaning. Thus the technical vocabulary of the new philosophy of nature became metaphorical through and through, a fact which was easily forgotten and often painfully rediscovered at later stages of the history of science when new linguistic crises emerged.

But the Greeks also discovered that the Book of Nature could be read in another way, in which its internal connections were described in a different language. Nothing allows us to doubt the unanimous tradition that the Pythagoreans performed acoustic experiments that disclosed an unexpected connection between the intervals of the musical scale and the integer numbers of mathematics. For instance, if the length of a string is halved, the note it produces is raised by an octave; if it is reduced to two-thirds, the note is raised by a fifth, and so on. These relationships must be "necessary", since they appear in all circumstances. It follows that there are necessary connections in nature which can be ascertained only by mathematical methods and expressed only in a mathematical language, a lesson that science has never since completely forgotten. This new insight led the Pythagoreans to a grandiose attempt to reconstruct the whole universe on the basis of the theory of integers. In this they failed, although we are still reminded of their program by expressions like the "harmony of the spheres", which refers to the Pythagorean effort to account for the speeds of the planets by means of the same mathematical proportions they had discovered in music. But the important point is that they discovered an alternative to the metaphorical discourse on nature. For, in the mathematical account of music, there were no metaphors. The length of a string is not an obscure symbol of something else. It can be measured by a simple ruler. Similarly, the interval between the notes can be ascertained by anyone who has an ear for music.

Thus the Book of Nature might be read either in a metaphorical or in a mathematical language, or in a combination of these two idioms. Out of this insight emerged three major scientific traditions which have competed over the ages for the place of honor in natural philosophy.

The Three Great Traditions

The first of these traditions may be properly named after Plato who was familiar with the Pythagorean discoveries in physics at the same time as he was deeply impressed by the spectacular development of Greek mathematics and the ability of mathematics to produce true propositions by means of reason alone. But he was also influenced by the Eleatic doctrine that Being, that which really is, must be absolutely unchanging. Consequently, the phenomena of this world of the senses could be nothing more than mere appearances, imperfect, material representations of the unchanging "ideas" and "forms" which inhabit a "separate", immaterial world, the truth of which is accessible to reason alone. Among the perfect "forms" are the objects of mathematics which are only crudely recalled in the shapes of material things, as the perfect circle is recalled by the rugged rim of a wheel. This implies that nature must be open to a mathematical description in the way that pre-existing mathematical "forms" or structures, known to reason alone, are used to discover the properties of material phenomena. For instance, that matter is composed of four primary elements called fire, air, water, and earth is said to follow from the geometrical properties of the five regular polyhedra,[12] or, in another account, from certain algebraic relationships between numbers or magnitudes.[13] In other words, Plato's thought implied a philosophy of nature in which mathematics played a role *a priori*, as a system of purely intellectual truths to which the description of nature had to conform quite independently of sense experience or experiment.

In the Aristotelian tradition we meet with a very different intuition of reality. For Aristotle there was no "separate" world of ideas to contemplate. Ultimately all knowledge was supposed to derive from experience, as the thousands of impressions on the senses are processed by the abstracting and inductive faculties of the mind, so that the "forms" that are inherent in the very objects in nature are brought to light. Also mathematical forms are disclosed *a posteriori* by studying material objects from a particular point of view, which abstracts from their physical material content and concentrates on such properties as number, size, or shape. Further abstraction leads to more general "metaphysical" principles that can be applied to everything. Among them the notions of "cause" and "effect" serve as the means of ascertaining the necessary connections in nature. "Any intellectual knowledge", said Aristotle, "deals with causes and principles"[14] and "the object of philosophical research is the causes of the phenomena".[15] A complete account of a phenomenon presupposes that one can identify its material, formal, efficient, and final causes. If there are events to which no cause can be ascribed, they happen by "chance" and fall outside the realm of scientific explanation. This was one of the reasons why Aristotle rejected the hypothesis that the random motions of atoms in a void were at the base of everything, as the atomists had proposed. This conception of science as a quest for causal explanations has dominated science ever since; but before it is taken for granted, it is worth remembering that its fundamental concept originated in the metaphor of *aitia* . But is the Book of Nature really written in a metaphorical language? Moreover, this concept of science ignored the problem of chance which was swept under the carpet from where it was destined to reappear much later with troublesome difficulties in its wake.

Historians of philosophy have sometimes been inclined to place any philosopher or scientist in either the Platonic or the Aristotelian tradition, but this view is too simplified, for there was also a third way of approaching nature. It was first exemplified by the acoustic research of the Pythagoreans and was later brought to perfection in Archimedes's mechanical investigation on the equilibrium of bodies under gravity. Also the astronomy of Ptolemy's *Almagest* belonged to this tradition, which may properly be called Archimedean. It is characterized by being both mathematical and empirical; but it does not apply mathematics *a priori*, as Plato would have it, but *a posteriori* and as a tool for discovering relationships in nature on the basis of observation or experiments. On the other hand it is not concerned with causal explanations as required by Aristotle. Consequently, it formed an independent, separate method of reading the Book of Nature in the language of mathematics. The history of science shows how fruitful it has been. It has from the very beginning produced insights which it would have been impossible to obtain in any other way, and its results have usually withstood the test of time very well. The Archimedean law of the lever is still valid in all its metaphysical nakedness. This gives rise to problems to which we shall return in later contexts.

The Demise of the Gods

The question must now be: Did the Greeks succeed in carrying out the great program of creating a non-mythological account of the phenomena of nature? Considering the development of Greek science from the first cosmological speculations of the Ionian philosophers to, for instance, the great synthesis of theoretical astronomy in Ptolemy's *Almagest* seven hundred years later, the answer must be yes. And, even if other sciences did not rise to the same heights, one must admit that the Greeks were, in fact, able to draw a comprehensive picture of the whole cosmos from which all mythological language was removed, or at least banned to fringe subjects like alchemy or Hermetic philosophy. The price of this success was paid by Greek religion. What happened to the gods of nature? Already in the fifth century B.C. Herodotus was aware of the direction in which the wind was blowing. Describing the great gorge through which the river Peneus drains the plain of Thessaly he noticed that

> The Thessalonians say that Poseidon made this passage whereby the Peneus flows, and this is reasonable, for whosoever believes that Poseidon is the shaker of the earth and that rifts made by earthquakes are the handiwork of this god, will judge from the sight of this passage that it is of Poseidon's making, for it is an earthquake, as it seems to me, that has riven the mountains asunder.[16]

This illustrates the situation in a nutshell. The rustic Thessalonians were not prepared to abandon the mythological explanation in favor of a new philosophy of which they may still have been ignorant, but Herodotus was sufficiently conversant with the new mode of thinking to ascribe the phenomenon to an immanent cause in nature itself. Poseidon was rapidly losing his status as an explanatory principle in geology.

Herodotus was tactful enough not to underline this conclusion, but others were less reticent. Already the Miletian philosopher Anaximenes had launched an attack on the traditional religion. He "did not deny that there were gods, or pass them over in silence. Yet he did not believe that air (the fundamental substance in his philosophy) was made by them, but rather that they arose from air".[17] Here the usual view is turned upside down. The gods do not explain nature but are themselves explained by it. In Heraclitus of Ephesus the "divine" is a kind of unifying principle called *logos* which permeates all phenomena as the ground of the rational order of the world.[18] This *logos* is encountered neither "by praying to statues"[19] nor by religious ceremonies, for the secret rites practiced among men are celebrated in a shameful way.[20] Accordingly both temple worship and mystery religions are illusory. In the same vein Xenophanes reproved the "theologians", Hesiod and Homer, "for what they had said about the gods . . . attributing to them everything that is a shame and a reproach among men, stealing and committing adultery and deceiving each other".[21] Here the philosophical rejection is accompanied by a moral condemnation of the behavior of the gods according to the myths. Xenophanes also ridiculed theological anthropomorphism in the most scathing terms:

> Mortals consider that the gods are born, and that they have clothes and speech and bodies like their own . . . The Ethiopians say that their gods are snub-nosed and black, the Thracians that theirs have light blue eyes and red hair,[22] adding that if cattle and horses or lions had hands or were able to draw, . . . horses would draw the form of their gods like horses, and cattle like cattle.[23]

Thus there was plenty of criticism. The gods had no explanatory value in the philosophy of nature. They were products of nature itself, or they were created by man in his own image and, consequently, as immoral as mortal men and women. So both the new conception of nature and heightened moral consciousness worked together to create a kind of religious vacuum. Some philosophers drew far-reaching consequences from this critical assessment of religious belief. A few ended up as full-fledged atheists, like Epicurus and Lucretius. The fact they were also supporters of the atomistic philosophy led others to believe that atomism as such was tainted with atheism, a somewhat hasty conclusion which has survived in some circles until today. Other philosophers made conscious attempts to fill the vacuum by exploring ways and means of making the new philosophy of nature the foundation of a new and more refined concept of god within the framework of a non-mythological universe. The fundamental condition for such attempts was laid down already by Xenophanes who claimed, in connection with his attack on religious anthropomorphism, that if there be a god he must be

> . . . one god, greatest among gods and men, in no way similar to mortals in body or in thought.[24]

In other words, only a monotheistic religion would be compatible with a scientific outlook.

Reconstructing God

This condition was not fulfilled by the philosophical theology which Plato developed in the *Timaeus*. It had the force of a story or myth about how the universe came into being when a "demiurge", or world-architect, established a cosmic order out of an original chaos in which "all things were in a state devoid of reason (*alogos*) or measure (*ametros*)".[25] He first made a world-soul, with the result that the world came into existence "as a living creature endowed with soul and reason owing to the providence of God."[26] Then followed the creation of a number of lesser gods, among whom were Gaia (earth) and Uranus (heaven), as well as Zeus and other members of the traditional Olympic pantheon. This made it possible to uphold divine worship in the old way with a multitude of gods. Now all the lesser gods were produced by the demiurge, who is sometimes called "god" pure and simple. But this is hardly enough to make the system monotheistic. At any rate, the demiurge was not identical with the supreme force of the universe, nor with the idea of The Good. He had to act in accordance with the pre-existing and eternal ideas of which the world of nature is only an imperfect imitation. It is no wonder that the demiurge remained a strange and abstract deity to whom no altar was ever erected.

A much more coherent attempt to found the idea of God on a philosophical basis was made by Aristotle, who was not only a "philosopher" in the modern sense of the word, but also one of the greatest scientists of the ancient world. His school in Athens, the Lyceum, was a real research institution, housing not only an important library, but also a great collection of zoological specimens from many different countries, some of them supplied by his pupil, Alexander the Great. This enabled him to lay the foundation for zoology as a separate science of nature[27] in a great *Historia Animalium* in which he described several hundreds of species, classified according to a system some of whose features have survived until today.[28] This familiarity with scientific research was the background of his insight into the fundamental role of sense experience and his view of nature as an interconnected whole bound together by causal connections. This was also the point of departure for his theology, which is the first example in history of the attempt to trace a road from nature to God by strictly logical means.

To summarize his argument, Aristotle reasoned as follows: The general causality in nature means that any change of a natural substance is caused by something else which is again caused by something else, and so on. It follows (with a very anachronistic illustration) that if we could make a metaphysical movie of the world with a film that is sensitive to causes, we would see a multitude of interacting causes which succeed each other as long as the world exists. Logically it is quite possible that such a chain of causal relations would stretch from an infinite past into an infinite future. This means that Aristotle's own belief in the eternity of the world cannot be refuted on philosophical grounds. But this is not the point of the argument, for, even if we did not make a movie of the universe on our special film, but only an instantaneous picture or "still" showing its appearance at a definite moment of time, we would still see an interconnected network of causes. Now it is a general principle of Greek thought, admitted by almost all philosophers, that what actually exists cannot be infinite. Therefore, at any given moment the number of actually existing causes must be finite. Since they are all interconnected, they can be arranged and sorted out in such a way that one particular cause is singled out as the "first" or most fundamental (in order, not necessarily in succession) upon which all the others must depend.

About this First Cause Aristotle has quite a lot to say. It must be unchanging, for otherwise it would itself have a cause and so it would not be the "first" in the universal network. It must also be immaterial, since everything in the material world is subject to change. It is, in fact

> . . . an eternal substance, which is unmoved and separated from all things that can be perceived by the senses. . . It cannot have extension, but must be without parts and indivisible . . . impassible, and immovable, but imparting motion during an infinite duration of time.[29]

So the First Cause is also the Prime Mover of the world;[30] and, since motion is a fact revealed by the senses, the Prime Mover must exist by necessity, a being unable to be otherwise than it is. Consequently, it is also perfect and thus the ultimate object of desire, or the "Supreme Good". And, since nature operates for a purpose, the Prime Mover must also be intelligent. Separate, immovable, intelligent, good, and the cause of everything else. "Such is the principle upon which heaven and earth are suspended." Being eternal it is divine, and Aristotle does not hesitate to call it "God" and to describe his Metaphysics accordingly as "theology".[31]

Aristotle's attempt to unite a scientific and a religious view of the world was a remarkable achievement. The challenge to religion of the new philosophy of nature was here countered by the scientific deduction of the existence of one single, eternal being as the ultimate source of all events in nature. All mythological or anthropomorphic elements were excluded as Xenophanes had demanded. But one cannot help asking whether Aristotle's god was more than a philosophical construction? Would he be able to satisfy the demands of a truly religious mind? There can be no doubt that the author of the majestic order of the universe might inspire both awe and love in the human soul. But could human beings also be loved by the Prime Mover so that there could be a mutual relationship between god and man? Was it enough to be eternal in order to be truly "divine"? There is some indication that Aristotle himself was not really convinced by what he had achieved. At least we know that in his last will he made provision for the erection of statues of Zeus Soter and Athena Soteira in his native city of Stagira,[32] thereby recognizing that the old religion contained something which his own theology had been unable to deliver.

Science and Wisdom

We now wish to comment on the philosophical status of Aristotle's argument. An admirable feature of his proof of god is that it began in the concrete world of human experience like any other scientific construction. But as such it was tied to Aristotle's general idea of science as a quest for causal links in nature. Not surprisingly it belonged, therefore, to what has been called the Aristotelian tradition and was metaphysical through and through. Now Aristotle knew perfectly well that there was another approach to the phenomena of nature. He explicitly referred to a number of disciplines "that are more physical than mathematical even if they combine both disciplines, such as optics, music, and astronomy".[33] In other words, he admitted the existence of an Archimedean approach, even though he lived a hundred years before Archimedes, since he recognized that phenomena could be connected *a posteriori* by means of mathematical relationships. But of this approach there is no trace in his theology. This raises the question as to why Aristotle consciously ignored the mathematical approach to nature when he tried to determine its ultimate source?

In order to find an answer to this riddle we must consider the whole
scientific movement in Hellas in a wider perspective, remembering that the new
philosophy of nature was not hailed by all and sundry as the way to that true
wisdom which must be the ultimate aim of the philosopher. In fact, there were
thinkers of the first order who nourished serious objections to the scientific
discourse as such. Among them had been Socrates, who in the immortal
conversation he had with his friends on the day of his execution, revealed that

> . . . when I was young . . . I was tremendously eager for that kind
> of wisdom which they call the investigation of nature. I thought
> it was a glorious thing to know the causes of everything, why
> each thing comes into being, and why it perishes, and why it
> exists, and I was always unsettling myself with such questions as
> these: Do heat and cold, by a sort of fermentation, bring about the
> organization of animals, as some people say? Is it the blood, or
> air, or fire, by which we think?

To such fundamental questions on the origin of life and human consciousness
there seemed to be no answers, a fact for which Socrates, in the first instance,
blamed himself with his usual irony:

> I investigated the phenomena of heaven and earth until finally I
> made up my mind that I was by nature totally unfit for this kind
> of investigation.[34]

So Socrates was not clever enough to become a scientist who searched for
a material cause for everything in the tradition of the first Ionian philosophers.
However, this was not the only reason for his disappointment as we can see from
the next passage of his story.

> One day I heard a man reading from a book by . . . Anaxagoras,
> that it is the mind that arranges and causes all things . . .

This program of explaining matter in terms of mind seemed more promising than
the materialistic attempts of the earlier philosophers, and

> . . . I was delighted to think that I had found in Anaxagoras a
> teacher of the cause of things quite to my mind, and I thought he
> would tell me whether the earth is flat or round and, when he had
> told me that, would go on to explain the cause and the necessity
> of it.

But Socrates did not want a mere description of nature. He also searched for a philosophy which comprised an ethical view of the world, wishing that Anaxagoras

> . . . would tell me the nature of the best, and why it is best for the earth to be as it is, and if he said that the earth was in the center, he would proceed to show that it is best for it to be in the center.[35]

However, once again disappointment set in when Socrates discovered that even Anaxagoras's idealistic point of departure was unable to satisfy his desires; but this time Socrates was not ready to take the blame himself, for

> . . . as I went on with my reading I saw that the man made no use of intelligence, and did not assign any real causes for the ordering of things, but mentioned as causes air and ether and water and many other absurdities.[36]

So here Anaxagoras fell back on the material causes of the Ionians. In the following argument Socrates does not deny the existence of such causes, but he denies that they give any ultimate explanation. With deadly irony he makes it clear that it may, of course, be said that he is sitting in his prison because his body is so composed of bones and sinews that it is able to sit. But this is to ignore the real causes of his imprisonment

> . . . which are that the Athenians decided that it was best to condemn me, and therefore I have decided that it was best to sit here, and that it is right for me to stay and undergo whatever penalty they order.[37]

The fact that this was said on the eve of his death shows how important it was for Socrates to leave behind the message that the natural philosophers were on the wrong track when they did

> . . . not look for the power which causes things to be now placed as it is best for them to be placed . . . giving no thought to The Good which must embrace and hold together all things.[38]

Thus Socrates's intellectual testament summarized his personal experience by maintaining that the study of nature is of no avail in the human quest for wisdom. Science may or may not be able to account for the structure of the material world, but it is forever unable to decide "what is the best", and it cannot reach out to The Good. So when all is said and done the scientific enterprise is

irrelevant to the highest aspirations of man and one had better abandon it in order
not to get lost in the mire of the phenomena. Over the ages this opinion has been
echoed by numerous philosophers who have rightly stressed the primacy of the
spiritual life, but wrongly denied the relevance of the material world. Among
them was Soren Kierkegaard with his diatribe against the microscope as a useless
and even ridiculous instrument which is unable to disclose the spiritual nature of
things, with the corollary that the scientist is a lost soul

> . . . who lives in the most terrible manner of all, fascinating and
> astonishing all the world with his discoveries and ingenuity, but
> is unable to understand his own self.[39]

Here the connection is obvious, for Kierkegaard had written his thesis *On the
Concept of Irony* with particular reference to Socrates. But later the same attitude
gave   rise   to   the   fatal   distinction   between   *Naturwissenschaft*   and
Geisteswissenschaft, introduced by Wilhelm Dilthey,[40]   which has made
generations of thinkers blind to the fact that the study of the Book of Nature
teaches the human spirit a lesson which it cannot afford to ignore.

Saving Science at a Cost

Returning to Socrates one cannot deny that he had pointed to a problem
which cried aloud for an answer, and it can be argued that an essential part of
Aristotle's thought can be understood as an attempt to find a place for science
in the quest for wisdom. Aristotle loved scientific research and spent much of his
time on the exploration of the animal world. He expressed here and there in his
rather matter-of-fact writings an emotional engagement in the study of nature, a
fact which reveals something of his human character and the delight he felt when
a new page of the Book of Nature was opened for inspection.[41] Unlike Socrates
and his followers Aristotle recognized the scientific enterprise from the inside as
a noble and rewarding pursuit which was able to satisfy some deep and intense
cravings of the mind. But how would it be possible to save this spiritually fertile
enterprise from the onslaught?

Here we must remember Aristotle's fundamental view of science as a
quest for causes. How was this view compatible with the more general view of
philosophy as a quest for wisdom? The answer was found in the doctrine of final
causes. The wise man knows "what is best" only if he understands the purposes
of things and events. Therefore, science can lead to wisdom only if it is seriously
concerned with purpose. This was without doubt the deeper reason why Aristotle

insisted so strongly that the causal explanation of nature is incomplete if it does not include an account of the final causes of the phenomena. Aristotle knew very well that there are phenomena in nature to which it is difficult or impossible to assign any final cause. Nevertheless, he maintained that

> . . . although the physicist has to deal with both material causes and purposes, he is more deeply concerned with the latter. For purpose directs the moving causes that act upon the material cause, not the reverse.[42]

It follows that, only if science is able to locate the final causes in nature, can the scientific endeavor be related to the ultimate search for wisdom.

We are now approaching the crux of the matter, namely Aristotle's strong belief that mathematics has nothing to do with causality. Causes produce changes and must therefore themselves be able to change except for the First Cause. But mathematical forms are stable and unchanging entities. So the question arises:

> How a principle of motion, or the nature of The Good, could reside in immovable beings.[43]

Here "immovable beings" are the mathematical "forms" in the Platonic sense, that is, ideal and separate entities that cannot change because they are already perfect. Now in Aristotle's philosophy the mathematical forms are not separate, but they are imbedded in the material world; yet they are as stable and unchanging as in Plato's separate world of ideas. It follows that they can serve neither as causes in general nor as final causes in particular. Therefore, mathematics is unable to reveal purpose. In Aristotle's words, in "changeless beings"

> . . . one cannot admit the existence, neither of this principle of motion, nor of The Good as such. This is also why mathematics does not prove anything by this sort of cause, just as furthermore it proves nothing by [the concepts of] the Good and the Bad. . . . No mathematician makes allusion to such things.[44]

We can now discern the contours of Aristotle's answer to Socrates. He tried to protect natural philosophy from being attacked as irrelevant to wisdom by describing science as a discourse about the complete range of causes, including purpose as the final cause. But in order to achieve this he clearly felt obliged to sacrifice mathematics and, by implication, all the disciplines of mathematical physics of what has been called the Archimedean tradition. This was a notable achievement that without doubt contributed to promote the

Aristotelian concept of science among those who valued natural knowledge and wished to integrate it into a wider perspective that also included the notion of The Good. In this way natural knowledge could be applied to ethical considerations and value judgments which were obviously important for human life. But Aristotle's solution had the serious weakness that it left the mathematical discourse on nature out in the cold, by failing to appreciate its special possibilities of giving access to the extra-mental reality, and by risking to relegate it to either a harmless curiosity for slightly eccentric persons, or to a mere prerequisite for technological activities. In the end it would lead to the separation of the "Two Cultures" against which C.P. Snow entered his angry protest some years ago.[45] In a wider perspective the question still remains as to how it could be possible to negate the religious relevance itself of an approach to nature which at the same time opened one of the doors to the real world.

Envoi

This brief and most incomplete reflection on the emergence of science in the ancient world has led us along a long and winding road. It began when the Greeks replaced the myths about nature by their groping insight into the immanent connections in a cosmos of law, order, and beauty. They tried to express it in either a metaphorical or a mathematical language with three distinct conceptions of science as the lasting result. The multitude of gods lost their role as originators of phenomena and it dawned upon the philosophers that the new approach to nature presupposed only one God whose existence Aristotle tried to demonstrate on the basis of his scientific tenets; but he was also clearly inspired by a truly religious feeling of awe of the orderly and beautiful structure of the universe. More prophetic spirits underlined the notion of wisdom as the all-embracing goal of human activity and within that notion Aristotle made an attempt to make room for natural philosophy, having no serious use for mathematical physics and its particular connection with reality. Such were, in brief, the initial conditions for the period to follow in which the Greek reading of the Book of Nature was confronted with Christian revelation and the Book of Holy Scripture. This is the subject matter of the next lecture.

Notes

1.   In the words of a Medieval poet, John Gower (*Confessio Amantis,* ed. H. Morley [London, 1889] 351):

And thus the sunne is overall

> The Chefe Planete imperiall,
> Above him and beneath him thre
> And thus between them regneth he
> As he that hath the middel place
> Among the seven.

2.   Actually the metaphor has a long pre-history in antiquity, being popular in both the Mithras religion and before that in Stoic philosophy. See Cicero, *In Somnium Scipionis*, chapter 4:

> The Sun has its place in the middle as the leader, king, and governor of the other luminaries.

3.   Ita profecto tamquam in solio regali Sol residens circumagentem gubernat astrorum familiam. (N. Copernicus, *De revolutionibus orbium coelestium*, I, 10, facs. ed. fol. 9v.); Cf. William Shakespeare, *Troilus and Cressida*, Act I, Scene 3.

4.   Cicero, *De natura deorum* II, 34.

5.   See Th. Jacobsen, "The Cosmos as a State", in H. Frankfort *et al.*, *Before Philosophy* (London, 1949) 137-199.

6.   *Odyss.* XII, 371 ff.

7.   *Iliad* VII, 409 and XXIV, 27; cf. Hesiod, *Theogonia*, 266.

8.   In Plato, *Republic* II, 379 a. Also Aristotle referred to Homer, Hesiod and (the legendary) Orpheus as "the ancient writers who were concerned with theology" *Meteor.* 353 a 35.

9.   Hesiod, *Erga* 527.

10.   Herodotus, *Historia* II, 20-26.

11.   Cf. Herodotus, *Historia* I, 116 and *Odyss.* VI, 136.

12.   Plato, *Timaeus* 54c.

13.   *Ibid.*, 3lc.

14.   Aristotle, *Metaphysics* V, l; 1025 b.

15.   *ibid.*, I, 9; 992a.

16.   Herodotus, *Historia* VII, 129.

17.   St. Augustine, *De civitate Dei* VIII, 2.

18.   Sextus Empiricus, *Adv. math.* VII, 132.

19.   Aristocritus, *Theosophia* 68, Kirk and Raven Fr. 245.

20.   Clemens Alexandrinus, *Protrept.* 22.

21.   Diogenes Laertius IX, 18.

22.   Clemens Alexandrinus, *Stromata* V, 109 and VII, 22.

23.   *ibid.* V, 109.

24.   *ibid.*

25.   Plato, *Timaeus* 53a.

26.   *Ibid.* 30b.

27.   The Loeb Classical Library contains editions (with English translations)
       by A.L. Peck of the *Historia Animalium* I-III (London, 1965) , *De
       Partibus Animalium* (London, 1955) and the *De Generatione Animalium*
       (London, 1953).

28.   See M. Manquat, *Aristote naturaliste* (Paris, 1932).

29.   *Metaph.* XII, 8, 1073a.

30.   This aspect is more developed in *Phys.* VIII, 5, 256a.

31.   *Metaph.* XII, 7, 1072b.

32. Diogenes Laertius, *Vitae philosophorum* V, 16.

33. Aristotle, *Phys.* II, 2, 194a.

34. Plato, *Phaedon* 96a. The translation is from the Loeb Classical Library edition by H.N. Fowler (London, 1914).

35. *Phaedon* 97 b.

36. *Phaedon* 98 b.

37. *Phaedon* 98 e.

38. *Phaedon* 99 c.

39. *S. Kierkegaards Papirer*, VII (1), 129-134 (Copenhagen, 1915).

40. W. Dilthey, *Einleitung in die Geisteswissenschaft*, 1883.

41. See e.g. *De partibus animalium* I, 5, 644b.

42. *Phys.* III, 1, 200a; cf. *De partibus animalium* I, 1, where the final cause is said to be the *"logos* of the thing".

43. *Metaph.* II, 2, 996a.

44. *Ibid.*

45. C.P. Snow, *The Two Cultures and the Scientific Revolution* (Cambridge, 1959). On the ensuing debate see J. Thale, *C.P. Snow* (Edinburgh and London, 1964).

II. THE BOOK OF NATURE

The Coming of Christianity

In the previous lecture we met with the idea that a radically new insight must always be accompanied by a linguistic crisis like that which happened when the Greeks replaced the whimsical gods of nature by the idea of a necessary and immanent order permeating the whole universe. Another illustration of the same idea is provided by the coming of Christianity and its transformation from being an obscure Jewish sect into a world religion transcending all national and social frontiers. For the first Christians were in a situation similar to that of the first philosophers. They were convinced that they had obtained the insight that the birth, life, death, and resurrection of Jesus of Nazareth had marked a radical change in the relations between God and mankind. But there were no words to express this insight in an adequate way just as there had been no words enabling the philosophers to speak adequately about concepts like "necessity" or "causality" in nature. Consequently, even the apostles had to speak in metaphors which hinted at the truth without being able fully to convey it. In St. Paul we find a whole array of such ordinary words into which he tries to squeeze a new meaning. For instance, Jesus had brought "salvation" to mankind. This is a word borrowed from medical language where it means that the crisis was over and the patient on the way to recovery. But it could also be said that Jesus had "redeemed" the world; here St. Paul used a term from the courts of law where a slave could be redeemed and made into a free citizen by a certain legal procedure, usually including manumission and the payment of a ransom or "redemption". It was also possible to speak of a person's "justification" in Christ, using a word with a deep meaning in semitic languages and conveying the idea of the correct behavior of both humans and inanimate beings within the order established and willed by God. In Arabic the same idea is expressed by the word "islam".

In this way the key words of the Christian proclamation of the Gospel began their theological career as inadequate pointers to a new insight that really was ineffable and too deep to be described in words, something of which St. Paul was well aware when he spoke of the "foolishness" of the new faith in the eyes of the Greeks.[1] But in the course of time these words suffered the same fate as their counterparts in the Greek discourse on nature. Their metaphorical character was forgotten by the force of habit as the Christians became numerous and accustomed to this special vocabulary in their mutual discourse on the faith. Thus the linguistic crisis of early Christian theology was in many ways similar to that of early Greek philosophy. Perhaps we can take this as an indication that a truly new and important insight had come to light. History confirms this view, since both science and theology have been with us ever since, each of them playing its own special role in the formation of the culture in which we live. We shall now consider a few episodes in the long relationship between natural science and Christian theology. Here the Church has not always been on the side of the angels and there is no reason to forget, for instance, the Galileo affair. On the other hand such violent conflicts should not obscure the fact that deep below the surface of such tragic, but sporadic events there have always been invisible currents of interaction of a more positive nature. If they are ignored we shall end up with the hackneyed and indeed false picture of the enmity of science and religion. We shall now try to trace some of these currents; and even if it is impossible to deal with more than a few episodes of a history spanning almost two thousand years, this should be sufficient to show that science and faith have been able not only to live together, but also to establish an intimate relationship from which they have both profited.

Science and the New Testament

Let us begin the investigation in the first Christian century with the writings of the New Testament since they are practically the only source of information about the intellectual life of the Church in the making. Here we may be puzzled by the fact that there are extremely few allusions to the physical nature of the world. There is no reason to believe that the apostles and evangelists were ignorant of the principal features of the Greek cosmos. We can also be sure that, if they had found the Greek discourse on nature to be incompatible with the message of the Gospel, they would have said so, considering the vehemence with which they attacked pagan morals. Consequently, we must conclude that the absence of a tract on cosmology from the New Testament is evidence that the first Christian writers found no reason to quarrel with the fundamental tenets of Greek science.

This argument *ex silentio* might be confirmed by a comparison between some of the central elements of the Christian faith on the one side, and the principal suppositions of Greek natural philosophy on the other. First and foremost Christianity was a strictly monotheistic religion like the Judaism out of which it emerged. When the faithful in Corinth worried about eating meat bought from pagan temples St. Paul reminded them that

> . . . even if there are so-called gods, be it in heaven or upon earth,
> as there be many gods and many lords [in the pagan world], to us

there is but one God of whom all things are and we in Him, and
one Lord Jesus Christ by whom all things are and we by Him.[2]

Consequently, the old gods of nature were illusory so that a mythological
discourse on nature would be as impossible in a Christian context as in Greek
philosophy.

Secondly, from its Judaic origin Christianity inherited also the belief that
the one God is the Creator of the World. This was common ground and there was
no special reason to stress it when Jewish audiences were addressed, as when St.
Stephen spoke to the Council of Jerusalem[3] or when Paul preached in the
synagogue in Antioch.[4] But when the Apostle lectured in Athens he felt obliged
to explain that "God made the world and all things therein".[5] This would hardly
shock the philosophers on the Areopagos who were scandalized only when St.
Paul went on to proclaim the resurrection of the dead.

On the other hand the Greeks would easily have misunderstood St. Paul's
talk about creation which did not refer to philosophical considerations of what
happened "in the beginning". What he had in mind was much more the mystery
of a "new creation" of mankind as a result of salvation in Christ, that is, the
liberation of humanity from the rule of sin. We remember that Old Testament
theology in general had also refused to develop cosmological theories, so that
emphasis might be placed on the "negative" aspect of the doctrine of creation,
namely, the denial that man had any part in the constitution of the universe[6] or
any title to its glory.[7]

From the Old Testament Christianity also took over the belief in God's
transcendence. When St. John said simply that: " No man had ever seen God",[8]
this implied that God was not identical to any phenomenon in nature, however
impressive and awe-inspiring it might be. Nevertheless, God had left a certain
imprint on this world, for, as St. Paul wrote to the Romans

> . . . that which may be known of God is manifest to them for God
> has shown it to them. For the invisible things about him are
> clearly seen from the creation of the world, being understood by
> the things that are made, even His eternal Power and Godhead.[9]

This was also the belief of the Stoics,[10] but the fact that it was so strongly
expressed in the New Testament became immensely important for the future
relations between science and faith. It meant that something about God could be
read in the Book of Nature in a way that is not clearly indicated and, therefore,
has to be explored. So, if there is a road from nature to God, then it can at least

be said that it must follow the path of our knowledge, not that of our ignorance. Gaps in natural knowledge are no loopholes for faith in God, and barriers on the scientific frontier cannot serve as bastions for Christian belief.

We seem to have arrived at a paradox. On the one hand the phenomena of nature are not divine; on the other, they testify to their divine origin in God. The Prologue to the Fourth Gospel pointed to a solution when it said that:

> In the beginning was the *logos*, and the *logos* was with God, and the *logos* was God. All things came into being through Him, and without Him not one thing came into being.[11]

This passage is difficult to understand without a careful interpretation of the Greek. The crux of the matter is the double meaning of the word *logos*. This term could mean the ordinary spoken words; but these were usually denoted by the term *rhemata* which is also current in the New Testament and used there, for instance, about the words Jesus spoke with his human voice. But *logos* could also denote the unspoken thought or reason behind the spoken word, or even the reason behind everything. Thus Heraclitus had used it about some kind of unifying substratum at the bottom of all phenomena[12] and in Stoic philosophy it denoted a universal "principle" of rationality that is immanent in nature itself, in contradistinction to the Platonic rationality that was derived from the "separate" world of "ideas" or archetypes.[13] Now there can be no doubt that the author of the Gospel used *logos* instead of the common term *rhema* because he wished to express something which *rhema* was unable to convey. This was the idea that the world had come into being according to rational principles and, therefore, must possess an immanent rationality; but that was precisely the basic supposition of Greek science. Moreover, he asserted that this rationality was of divine origin. It was not only with God; it was God. Consequently, God is not only transcendent and separate from nature. He is also immanent in the world by way of its inner rationality. This idea would have also been understood by a philosopher. But when the Evangelist went on with the amazing assertion that the divine *Logos* "became flesh and dwelt among us"[14] in the person of Jesus of Nazareth, this was no doubt another instance of the foolishness of the Christian faith. Nevertheless, the logos-christology was destined to be of momentous importance as linking the scientific assumption of the rationality of nature with the deepest and most precious mystery of the Christian faith, the belief that God had at one time become incarnate in the human world. To believe in Christ as the divine *Logos* made it impossible to negate that the world was open to scientific exploration.

Thus the first Christian literature contained a number of guidelines for a Christian reading of the Book of Nature. There was one God only whose own rationality had become immanent in His created world from which a certain "natural knowledge" of God might be gathered. This explains why the New Testament writers left Greek science alone, since, whether or not they were aware of it, they simply shared its fundamental assumptions.

Prelude in the Early Church

A much more conscious interaction between Christian faith and Greek philosophy of nature was mediated in the next four centuries by the Fathers of the Church whose manifold achievements we must deal with here in a much too brief and cavalier way. Of course, the Fathers were not scientists, but churchmen and theologians dedicated to the great work of proclaiming the Gospel to the whole world and of taking care of the affairs of the Church. They had no call to explore the physical universe for its own sake, and what they had to say about nature had usually an occasional character. The faithful had to be warned against unacceptable elements of pagan thought. Philosophical objections to the faith had to be refuted and the very contents and implications of the faith itself had to be explored. Let us here consider a few such cases.

The belief in astrology was universally rejected and all the Fathers led a most resolute campaign against it. Divination and magic were branded as arts of the devil. As a child of the "Chaldaean" worship of the stars astrology in particular was condemned as idolatry, even after it had been presented in the form of a non-religious pseudo-science in the second century. This was realized at last by St. Augustine who changed the polemics accordingly, arguing that, in contrast to astronomy, the art of astrology was simply unable to make true predictions so that it must be rejected as superstitious.[15] This understanding gradually penetrated Christian thought and for several centuries astrology was at a very low ebb. Before this sensible solution was reached the Biblical account of the Star of Bethlehem had been a difficulty. Did it not prove that predictions by the stars was possible? Around AD 200 Origen replied that all diabolic arts belonged to the old dispensation and became obsolete with the coming of Christ, astrology having performed its last and final service by announcing the birth of its victor.[16]

Whereas astrology could be discarded as a surviving superstition, the main body of Greek thought presented a more serious problem. On the one hand St. Paul had fulminated against the "wisdom of this world"[17], on the other he had commended "whatsoever things that are true . . ., honest . . ., just . . ., lovely and of good report".[18] Consequently a dialectical attitude was necessary and it became imperative both to try the spirits and to find a reason why pagan thought might be true and honest, a question that occupied the Apologetic Fathers of the second century. One possible answer was based on a rather fanciful reconstruction of intellectual history (already proposed by the Jewish philosopher Philo who was a contemporary of St. Paul) according to which the teaching of Moses had been mysteriously transmitted to the Greek philosophers. Another solution was founded on the Johannine *logos* christology from which St. Justin the Martyr drew the conclusion that the divine logos had already illuminated human minds before the time of Christ, so that "all authors have had a glimpse of the truth because the seed of the *logos* was implanted in them."[19]

This immensely fruitful idea opened the door for Christians to read the Book of Nature together with Gentiles; but at the same time the other great book gave rise to serious questions. The divine authority of the Bible was unquestioned in the Church, but what would happen if it contradicted the Book of Nature? Since the two "Books" originated from the same author it became imperative to establish that such contradictions were only apparent. One way of removing them was based on the exegetical principles worked out in Alexandria towards the end of the second century, according to which the divine message was not always conveyed by the literal meaning of the text; there was also an allegorical and an even deeper mystical sense which was the true word of God.[20] The literal sense might be wrong, as when Scripture speaks of God's "hands" or "feet" or "voice".[21] Such anthropomorphic language is unavoidable, but it is also misleading. St. Augustine used this method to save the spherical shape of the universe from the Biblical assertion that God had spread the heavens like a tent, an expression which he considered to be only an allegory. He also warned against discarding reason on the basis of Holy Scripture,[22] declaring bluntly that if a Biblical passage seems to be absurd it is either "because the text is faulty, or because the interpreter is mistaken, or because you have not understood it".[23] By such means it became possible to maintain a balance between the two Books, although there were cases in which the literal sense prevailed in an unfortunate and unnecessary way. Thus most of the Fathers clung to a literal interpretation of the "Waters above the Heavens" of ancient Jewish cosmology (Genesis 1,7; cf. Ps. 19,5) with the result that the Greek universe was equipped with a sphere of "celestial water" outside the firmament.[24] But this was rather an exception to the general rule that the Greek account of the universe was not seriously disturbed by the reading of the Bible as the Word of God, properly understood. In fact, serious difficulties in this field did not arise until the time of Galileo.

The Doctrine of Creation

More serious and more full of consequences than these details was the encounter between Greek thought and the belief in God, the Creator of heaven and earth, as expressed in the very first article of the Apostolic Creed. It was one thing to believe in the *fact* of creation; it was a very different matter to explore the *act* of creation, since theology had always regarded what happened "In the beginning" as an impenetrable secret of God. But, since the physical origin of the world was a standard problem of Greek philosophy from its very infancy, it was difficult for Christian thinkers to ignore it completely. In fact, the Fathers had quite a lot to say about it, and on this point they ventured into speculations with far reaching consequences for some of the most fundamental concepts of natural philosophy. Already among the Apologetic Fathers we can discern a highly significant development.

Both St. Justin[25] and St. Clement of Alexandria,[26] as well as the unknown author of the Letter to Diognetus,[27] described creation as an act in which the divine *logos* established law and order in an original chaos of confused, pre-existing matter. Since this chaotic matter was uncreated it was also eternal. But in Greek thought that which is eternal is *ipso facto* divine. Consequently, this theory of creation presupposed two divine beings, eternal matter and God. But this was incompatible with a monotheistic religion. Therefore, Origen broke right away with the traditional belief in the eternity of matter. For him creation was not simply the ordering of a chaos according to a divine plan executed by the divine *logos* as a kind of Platonic demiurge. It was the calling into being of something that did not previously exist.[28] This was the famous doctrine of *creatio ex nihilo*. It took quite a long time before this apparently absurd doctrine was assimilated. This was not only because it seemed strange to minds schooled in Greek thought, but also because it raised ethical problems. If matter is created by God it was impossible to consider it as the root of all evil, as many philosophers had done, and as the widespread Manichaean heresy incessantly proclaimed.

The doctrine of *creatio ex nihilo* had equally startling consequences in another field. Since the Bible said "In the beginning", one could assume that the world came into being a finite time ago. One could even try to determine its age by means of chronological statements in the Old Testament, which seemed to indicate that creation took place some 4000 years before the incarnation. There could be no philosophical objection to the idea that time was finite, but it raised a theological problem which Origen expressed by asking: "If the world had a beginning in time, then what did God do before the world began?"[29] Was the eternal and immutable God "idle" from all eternity, only to become "active" a little more than 4000 years ago? This was a preposterous idea, but it was difficult to find good reasons for rejecting it. Origen's own answer was that before the

present world was created God was occupying Himself with another world which
disappeared when our world was created, just as our world would be succeeded
by another, and another again, until the completion of time when God would be
all in all.[30] But this idea of a succession of worlds seemed too close to the
astrological idea of a "Great Year" to become acceptable, and it earned Origen
his later reputation of being a heretic (a judgement which seems to have been
undeserved). But the problem remained.

Time and Eternity

The doctrine of creation also gave rise to problems in the philosophical
field thanks to the generally accepted Aristotelian notion of time as the "number
of motion"[31] or that by which motion is measured. Now motion clearly
presupposes a moving body. Consequently, there could be no time before the
creation of the world. Time must be something that came into being together
with matter. But if this happened a finite time ago, how could God then be called
eternal, that is, existing during an infinity of time? And how could God be
"always called Lord and yet have no creature to be Lord over" as St. Augustine
formulated the problem.[32] Such perplexing questions revealed how difficult it
was to speak of God in terms like "before" and "after" as these words were used
in ordinary language. Thus we have a new example of a linguistic crisis, and a
foreboding that a new insight was groping its way through a breakdown of
ordinary language.

The difficulty was clearly recognized by St. Gregory of Nazianzen in his
comment on the words by which God revealed Himself to Moses:

> I am [He] who am, not "who was" or "who shall be"; for "was"
> and "shall be" refer to our time and the changing natures; but He
> is an eternal being, and eternity is neither a time, nor part of a
> time, for it cannot be measured.[33]

Shortly afterwards the breakthrough came with St. Augustine who finally broke
with the Greek idea of eternity as an everlasting time. Time and eternity belong
to different categories, and Augustine states

> . . . the extent of time is produced by nothing else than a
> succession of many moments which cannot pass simultaneously.
> But quite contrary there is nothing successive about eternity.
> Everything is present, whereas time cannot be present all at
> once.[34]

Therefore, there is no "before" or "after" in God, and it makes no sense to ask what He did before our time came into being.

This notion of eternity as a non-temporal mode of existence was perhaps the most far-reaching implication of the monotheistic doctrine of *creatio ex nihilo*. Theology has cherished it ever since as one of the finest fruits of early Christian thought in its encounter with Greek philosophy. But it was still necessary to find an answer to Origen's question without resorting to the idea of a succession of separate worlds. In a way the separation of time and eternity would make this idea more acceptable from a purely philosophical point of view, since it would make it possible to imagine even an infinite number of worlds succeeding each other in time, without being for that reason eternal, but only "sempiternal", to use a word introduced later on to denote an infinity of time. In order to get rid of the idea of a succession of worlds St. Augustine had to bring out the big guns. Since he found nothing in the doctrine of creation that made this unacceptable idea impossible, it became necessary to mobilize the very core of the Christian faith, that is, the belief that Christ is not only the divine *logos* of creation, but also the redeemer of the world, whose redemption is absolutely final. Against the notion of an incessant repetition of history St. Augustine cried out:

> God forbid that we should ever believe this! For Christ died once for our sins and, rising again, dies no more (cf. Rom. 6,9) . . . And, after our resurrection "we shall be with the Lord always" (1.Thess. 4, 17).[35]

It is not easy to survey all the momentous implications of this appeal to the belief in salvation in Christ; perhaps they have not yet been fully disclosed. But the immediate consequence was that the myth of the Great Year and the Eternal Return was banned from the Christian idea of history. The great Wheel of Fate was stopped in its meaningless rounds; for the history of the world was not just the story of the unfolding of the physical universe with humans as insignificant spectators. It was also the history of salvation. It had both a beginning and a goal. The passage of time had a fundamental significance, and there was room for that virtue of hope which Greek philosophy had ignored. This was a new insight, and it emerged in a theological context. But with only a little reflection we can see its implications also for the scientific discourse on the universe. Greek philosophy of nature did not take time seriously, since it always aimed at timeless truths and unchanging relationships. Therefore, the idea that time is important was, as it were, a kind of time bomb ticking away under the very foundation of that static reconstruction of nature, which the Greeks had developed, and which remained the unquestioned pattern of scientific thought for many centuries to come. We shall see later what happened when it finally exploded.

Preparing the Soil

While St. Augustine was pondering over time and eternity the ancient order of the world was already passing away. The Roman Empire disintegrated, and while Greek culture survived in the east, the western provinces came out of the turmoil as separate kingdoms ruled by peoples from the north. Out of this commotion emerged a new civilization which the historians of the Renaissance called the Middle Ages, while the philosophers of the Enlightenment delighted in describing it as one long period of repression during which both Scholasticism and the Inquisition tried to quench all innovative ideas in general and all scientific novelties in particular. It has taken a relatively small band of dedicated scholars more than a hundred years to eradicate this false and condescending picture which survives, nevertheless, both in the public mind and in various political ideologies. However, here we shall not go into the history neither of medieval science, nor of its rediscovery, but we shall only reflect upon a few points of general importance to the history of the Book of Nature in this long period.

The initial conditions were indeed poor. The network of Roman schools fell into ruin and the Greek language disappeared in the west. Consequently the seminal, but never translated, sources of Greek science fell into oblivion. The only remaining supra-national institution was the Church which took charge of the remaining fragments of learning. But the Church was preoccupied with its proper mission, the enormous task of evangelizing the peoples of Europe, at the same time as it became inevitably involved in the establishment of a new social and political order. Consequently, the pursuit of scientific knowledge would be a matter of secondary importance, although the many small monastic and cathedral schools included a few elements of disciplines like cosmology, time reckoning and mathematics into their curricula. Nevertheless, there can be no doubt that the very proclamation of the Gospel was instrumental in preparing the soil in which a more scientific study of nature would eventually strike root. First and foremost, the missionary efforts of the Church implied that the non-mythological attitude to nature was implanted in all countries of Europe as they were converted to the Christian faith. In this process both the learned scholar and the common priest were engaged in the battle against the old gods of nature, a battle which had to be won before the work of the Greeks could be continued.

One of the few real scholars of the initial period of the Middle Ages (the so-called "Dark Ages") was Archbishop Isidore of Seville. In the beginning of the seventh century he first published a short manual, *De natura rerum*,[36] which formed a kind of first introduction to the universe for the beginning students of his school. As such it became the prototype of numerous similar books over the next four or five centuries. It was followed by a work of a very different scale, the huge encyclopedia: *Twenty Books on the Origin of Words*,[37] in which Isidore explained, sometimes in a very fanciful way, the etymologies of the key words of all theoretical and practical forms of knowledge. Historians have often misjudged this work, interpreting it only as a testimony to the scientific ignorance of its author. But Isidore's principal purpose was not to provide scientific information as such, but to show that all phenomena in nature and society could be described in a vocabulary from which all mythological elements had been ruthlessly removed or relegated to the realm of fables. It was no doubt a homespun and shaky etymology which led Isidore to derive the name of the Sun from *solus apparet*;[38] but the point is that he described the Sun only as a celestial body moving in a well defined orbit, while every reference to its divine status is carefully omitted. From this point of view Isidore's works stand out as an example of how a scholar could contribute to the cleansing of nature from the old beliefs. A particular illustration is his precise distinction between astronomy as a science and astrology as a superstition[39], a distinction which became normative for a long time into the future.

At this time of history very few people were able to read, so only a tiny fraction of the population would be directly affected by the written works of the scholars. But here the simple parish priests came to the assistance of their learned colleagues by hammering away, Sunday after Sunday, at the pagan heritage of their rude congregations. For instance, the author of the old *Anglo-Saxon Homilies* explained again and again the Christian doctrine of Creation and its implications:

> The heretics say that the devil created some creatures, but they lie.
> He can create no creatures for he is not a creator.[40]

This was against Manichaean and other beliefs in matter as the root of evil. But there is no evil except in the heart of man:

> All creatures, sun, moon and all stars, land and sea and cattle, all
> serve their Creator, because they perform their courses after God's
> direction. Wicked man alone . . . is the devil's thrall.[41]

Astrology in particular and the doctrine of Fate in general were forcefully rejected:

> Let this error depart from believing hearts that there is any destiny, excepting the Almighty Creator who provides life for every man by his merits. Man is not created for the stars, but the stars are created as a light by night for men.[42]

Therefore:

> Let us set our hope and happiness in the providence of the Almighty Creator who has placed all creatures in three things: that is, in measure, and in number, and in weight. Be to Him glory and praise ever to eternity. Amen.[43]

Repeated week after week such simple exhortations could not fail to make an impact. The old mythological concept of nature would slowly disappear or be driven under ground. And finally the day arrived when St. Francis of Assisi was able to give poetic expression to the new attitude in his wonderful *Canticle of the Sun*. Clearly a watershed had been passed. It was now possible to love nature in a new way and, as always, love casts out fear. There was nothing to fear from the phenomena of nature, for however impressive or perilous they were, they were ordained by God. Also there was no risk that the human soul might be debased or defiled by matter which was God's creation. Whereas the scholars of the Early Middle Ages had delighted in the manifold manifestations of nature as signs and symbols of something else, it was now possible to study them for their own sake, for the Book of Nature was not a heretical work. In this way the doctrine of creation contributed to the victory of a new attitude which no doubt paved the way for a renewed study of nature by removing any religiously founded objection to the exploration of its secrets.

Law and Contingency

While this new confidence in created nature was slowly captivating the minds of all believers, great and more spectacular events were happening in the more restricted world of the scholars. At long last practically all the principal works of ancient science were recovered in translations from Arabic and soon also from the original Greek.[44] Among them were the complete works of Aristotle whose doctrines now began to revolutionize the teaching of the schools and the new universities that emerged from them. Aristotle became known as "The Philosopher" pure and simple, and the traditional Platonism of the followers of

St. Augustine was forced to go on the defensive. The great scholastics, led by St. Albert the Great and St. Thomas Aquinas, were busily engaged in recasting Christian thought in an Aristotelian mould by using, for instance, Aristotle's deduction of the First Cause and Prime Mover to establish the existence of God as one of the "prolegomena" of the Christian faith and as a philosophical truth, clearly distinguishable from those higher truths that are known only because they are revealed by God. But also 13th century science profited by the contact with The Philosopher. Thus the Aristotelian principle of experience furthered the rediscovery of the experimental method which now produced new results in fields like optics and magnetism.[46]

However, in the middle of all this intellectual excitement some nagging questions remained. Was Aristotle not a pagan philosopher who could not be trusted in everything he had said? Had he not maintained that the world was eternal and that its history went in self-repeating cycles? And were there no other principles in nature than necessity and chance? Would his philosophy leave room for hope or love or prayer? Such questions made havoc in the universities, causing bitter quarrels between Averroistic scholars who wished to follow Aristotle to the very end, and other thinkers who refused to surrender the whole territory of reason to his authority. At last this confusion caused the higher authorities to intervene, and in 1270 and 1277 both Bishop Etienne Tempier of Paris and Archbishop Robert Kilwardby of Canterbury published lists of propositions which the masters in Paris and Oxford respectively were forbidden to teach as true. Most detailed was the Parisian *rotula* from 1277 containing no less than 219 such philosophical or theological errors.[47] We cannot analyze this list here in any detail, but its general tenor was a clear warning not to let the indispensable notion of necessity in nature infringe upon faith in God's divine freedom and almighty power, or upon the essential freedom of the human will. Thus a number of condemnations were aimed at the belief in astrology which was once again in the ascendent in all strata of society. Others denied that the eternity of the world could be proved in philosophy, or that God cannot move the heavenly bodies in another way than they are moved now.

More than anything else this intervention was a reminder that one should never use arguments beginning with words like: "God cannot . . . ", for the power of God is unlimited and His will is free to do what pleases Him. This might seem to destroy the fundamental idea of natural philosophy, that is, that there are truly necessary connections between the phenomena of nature. Consequently, it became necessary to reconsider the doctrine of creation in light of the freedom and omnipotence of God, a task to which scholars like John Duns Scotus and William of Ockham in the beginning of the 14th century devoted most of their energy and philosophical acumen. The result was a new and more profound insight into the contingent nature of the created world. This meant on the one hand that God had established the internal connections in nature in a definite way, which is necessary in the sense that it will never change because God upholds it. But, on the other hand, this definite order is contingent upon the Will of God in the sense that there could have been a different order of the world if God had so willed. This had obvious consequences for the philosophy of nature: The laws of nature are immutable because God does not change His mind, but they are not the only possible laws because God might have created a different universe. It follows, as an important corollary to this idea, that we cannot be sure that the laws formulated thus far by the philosophers are necessarily true. In particular, one cannot be sure that Aristotle has said the last word in physics or cosmology. On the contrary, one had to re-examine his statements with the notions of the divine freedom and power as guiding principles.

God and Space

This re-examination became a major program of the natural philosophy of the 14th century. As a single example we shall here consider only the new debate on the nature of space. In this area very little had been achieved since antiquity when Aristotle had defined the concept of *topos* or "place" as the boundary of material bodies.[48] It followed that where there is no matter, there can be no "place", so that the idea of an extended vacuum in nature is unthinkable. This view was taken over by the Fathers of the Church who drew the conclusion that "place" must have been created together with matter just as was supposed to have been the case for time. Now we have seen the Fathers answering the question: "What did God do before the creation of the world", by separating the notion of time from the notion of eternity. But the parallel question: "Where was God before He created heaven and earth?",[49] had not found any real answer since it was not very informative to say that God dwelt in himself and by himself.[50]

Here the problem rested until it was addressed again in light of the new emphasis on the power of God. In the 14th century Albert of Saxony conceded that God could annihilate everything within the sky, after which the sky would be a vacuum.[51]   Others, however, offered various experiments proving the physical impossibility of a vacuum inside the world. The decisive breakthrough came in the introduction to the large work, *De causa Dei contra Pelagianos et De virtute causarum*, by the Oxford scholar Thomas Bradwardine who died from the Great Plague just after his nomination to the see of Canterbury. Starting with the generally accepted belief that God is necessarily everywhere in the world and all its parts, he argued that God is also beyond the real world in a place, or in an imaginary, infinite void. This idea made it possible to call God truly immense and unlimited, and so a reply seems to emerge to the old questions of the Gentiles and the heretics: "Where is your God?" and "Where was God before the world [was]?". Now Aristotle had proved the world to be unique, finite, and spherical; but here the Aristotelians cannot be trusted because they seriously diminish and mutilate the divine and, indeed, omnipotent Power, as the Bishop of Paris had pointed out in 1277.[52]

It is possible that Bradwardine was led to this new idea by studying the Hermetic treatise, *Asclepius* (also called *De aeterno verbo*), from which he quoted the famous description of God as an infinite sphere whose center is everywhere and circumference nowhere. But it is significant that he argued for it with a direct reference to the condemnation of 1277 and in the context of the omnipotence of God. The result was a radical break with all previous views, since Bradwardine not only maintained that a vacuum can exist independently of bodies, but also that the universe must be infinite, although in a rather special sense. The material or "real" world was still supposed to form a finite spherical body; but outside this body there is an infinite and "imaginary" space. Why this empty space was called imaginary is nôt quite clear; perhaps it meant that it was without the ordinary three spatial dimensions, being closely connected with God who has no dimensions. A generation after Bradwardine the same idea was taken up in Paris by Nicole Oresme who definitely identified the imaginary, empty space with God.[53] In the following century an even greater step was taken by Nicolaus Cusanus (later he became a Cardinal) who clearly had an intuition of what is now called the general cosmological principle, namely, the assumption that the universe is everywhere structured in the same way, apart from local variations. His description of the earth as a "noble star" among innumerable similar bodies, rotating around different axes and moving through an infinite space, indicates that Cusanus regarded such a space as real.[54]

The Rise of Mathematical Physics

This sketch of the 14th century debate on space is sufficient to show how the theological idea of contingent creation was able to shake some of the cornerstones of Aristotelian cosmology and philosophy of nature. In the meantime, we have lost sight of the Archimedean tradition, understood as the idea that the Book of Nature is written in the language of mathematics. This idea was by no means absent in the Middle Ages, although it led a more quiet life and gave rise to much less intellectual commotion than the tenets of The Philosopher. Already in the 13th century Robert Grosseteste in Oxford taught that

The usefulness of considering lines, angles, and figures cannot possibly be exaggerated since it is impossible to know natural philosophy without them. They are absolutely valid [applicable] in the universe as a whole as also in its individual parts.[55]

Roger Bacon expressed himself even more strongly, calling

. . . mathematics a universal way to knowledge . . . which applies also to other sciences . . . since no science can be known without mathematics . . . The naked natural philosopher must know that he is ignorant and vacillating in almost any field if he is not previously instructed in mathematics.[56]

We are here far beyond the Aristotelian philosophy of mathematics and its role in science to which, for instance, Thomas Aquinas adhered in the same years.[57] Nevertheless, it would be wrong simply to place Roger Bacon and Robert Grosseteste within the Archimedean tradition, since they seem to have had no intention of abandoning the idea of science as a quest for causal relationships in nature.

On the other hand we have at least some evidence that in these very years the Aristotelian concept of science began to lose some of its sovereign status. Thus a rather obscure scholar by the name of Gerard of Brussels wrote a treatise, *De motu*,[58] in which he dealt with problems of motion in a purely kinematic way, without caring about forces as the causes of motion. He referred to the works of Archimedes in which physical problems were treated from the same point of view. This approach was no doubt stimulated by the new translation of the works of Archimedes made directly from the Greek about 1269 by the Dominican scholar William of Moerbeke. This gave the later Middle Ages easy access to the most important Greek works in mathematics and mathematical physics, a fact which has greatly changed our view of the scientific history of this period.[59]

In the 14th century this new trend appears in many scholars, several of whom were fellows of Merton College, Oxford. They asserted that the motion of a body may be described either *quoad causas* as a result of the moving forces, or *quoad effectus* without reference to such forces, but only in terms of space and time. This meant that kinematics was separated from dynamics as an independent part of mechanical science, although not in the Aristotelian meaning of the word science. Some highly significant results followed. Among them was the so-called "Merton relation" between time, velocity, and distance of a body moving with a constant acceleration. It was equivalent to the modern formulae, $s = gt^2$ and $v = gt$, which Nicole Oresme was also able to prove by a new graphical method of his own invention, and which was later used by Galileo to describe the free fall of bodies.

We cannot here follow the details of this important development of a purely mathematical discourse on one of the central problems in physics: how to describe the motion of bodies. But it is proper to notice that this new, and more or less Archimedean spirit, was also at work in the astronomy of Copernicus whose great work, *De revolutionibus orbium celestium* (1543), fits well into this mathematical tradition. Copernicus set out to remedy some of the alleged defects of Ptolemy's *Almagest* in which there were non-uniform circular motions which seemed objectionable from a philosophical point of view. At the same time there was no explanation of the strange "coincidence" that the annual motion of the Sun enters into the apparent motion of all the planets. The latter defect was removed by Copernicus by placing the Sun at rest in the middle of the universe, which was still supposed to be limited by the sphere of the fixed stars, at the same time as the earth became a planet revolving around the sun with a period of one solar year. The non-uniform motions were avoided by a system of planetary epicycles which was at least as intricate as that of Ptolemy. But the point is that all this was achieved in a purely mathematical way, just as in the Almagest, without any consideration of the moving forces in the solar system. Consequently, it is legitimate to place Copernicus's celestial kinematics in the Archimedean tradition together with its Ptolemaic predecessor. This is not to say that Copernicus regarded his system as a merely mathematical ploy to "save the phenomena" of the heavens in a new way. That he regarded it as a true description of physical reality appears, for instance, from his remark that it would be necessary to change the concept of gravity. Terrestrial gravitation could no longer be construed as a tendency to move towards the center of the world, for the earth was no longer there. But this was a secondary implication which does not invalidate the conclusion that the Copernican system emerged as another potent illustration of the power of the Archimedean approach to nature.

The Priesthood of the Scientist

While the mathematical discourse on nature matured and increasingly proved its ability to disclose hidden connections between phenomena, its theological implications remained unexplored. It is true that Roger Bacon had dreamed of a kind of unified description in mathematical terms of all sciences, including theology, in order to make the Christian faith more easily understandable to both Muslims and pagans. After him Ramon Lull also started an ambitious project of developing a universal calculus comprising all true theological and scientific propositions within a single logical scheme. But Roger Bacon's mathematical physics (mainly geometrical optics) remained rudimentary, and Ramon Lull's unfinished project suffered, among other things, from the erroneous idea that the Christian faith can be exhausted by a set of logical propositions, despite the metaphorical origin of the key words in the Christian proclamation. Moreover, these attempts were disregarded by the main stream of scholastic theology, in which the Aristotelian, metaphysical approach reigned supreme. It is true that this approach was challenged with great success in the field of logic by William of Ockham and his "nominalistic" followers; but it is also true that this did not lead to any new theological appraisal of natural science.[60]

Also the great pioneers of Renaissance science seem to have paid little attention to the possibility of moving the dialogue between theology and science into the mathematical or Archimedean domain. At least this was the case with Copernicus who was a good run-of-the mill Catholic, who spent his whole life as an administrator of the vast diocese of Ermland and drew his salary as a prebendary canon of Frombork Cathedral. But if his scientific achievements meant anything to his personal, religious convictions he told posterity nothing about it. Similarly Tycho Brahe was a professed Lutheran (as all Danish citizens had to be), but he hardly possessed a profoundly religious mind. His rejection of the Copernican system owed much to his failure to observe any annual parallax of the fixed stars. Yet he also maintained (as did Melanchthon before him) that the motion of the earth was incompatible with Holy Scripture, although it is difficult to say how much he was influenced by this argument.[61] Not until Kepler do we meet with a first-class scientist who seriously considered his scientific research in the light of his religious faith.

Like Tycho Kepler was a Lutheran, although he had reservations with respect to the Lutheran doctrine of the Eucharist. He also showed a strongly irenical attitude and believed that God would not condemn outright the heathen who do not believe in Christ. He advocated peace between Lutherans and Calvinists and fairness towards Catholics.[62] The same "ecumenical" spirit marks his scientific work in which he drew freely upon all the three major traditions. Since he was always a convinced Copernican, he tried in his first work, the *Mysterium Cosmographicum* (1596), to calculate the relative sizes of the Copernican orbits from the geometrical properties of the five regular polyhedra. This attempt to derive information on the universe from already known, purely geometrical structures was clearly in the Platonic tradition. It was a failure, but throughout his life Kepler remained deeply convinced that only mathematical methods can disclose the secrets of nature. Later in the *Astronomia Nova* (1609) he also failed to derive a circular orbit of Mars that would satisfy Tycho Brahe's (and his own) observations. This led him to consider the physical force that causes the planet to move. Assuming this force to come from the Sun and to be in the inverse ratio of the distance, he derived the relation which is now known as Kepler's Second Law. This way of determining an effect from its assumed cause was obviously an excursion into the Aristotelian tradition. Armed with the Second Law Kepler now returned to the problem of the orbit. After many cumbersome calculations, and driven by his respect for the empirical data, he at long last realized that the orbit must be elliptical, a result he then generalized to all the planets to establish what we call Kepler's First Law. Here he was on the Archimedean track, because the mathematical property of the orbit was not assumed *a priori*, but derived *a posteriori* from numerical observations. Some years later the Third Law emerged in a book called *Harmonices Mundi* (1619) which began with a long section on the mathematical theory of music in the Pythagorean tradition. Consequently, it has often been assumed that the Third Law came to light by applying musical theory to Copernican astronomy in a kind of updated version of the "harmony of the spheres". While it is true that Kepler here praised Pythagoras, a close reading of the text nevertheless reveals that the Third Law was discovered *a posteriori* by trial and error calculations which showed for all the planets a constant ratio, $T^2 : a^3$, where T is the period of revolution and a the semi-major axis. As an *a posteriori* deduction of a law from numerical data provided by observation this was clearly more in the Archimedean than in the Pythagorean or Platonic tradition.

No previous scientist had been able to carry to such perfection this type of mathematical approach to nature. More than any one else Kepler became the herald of a new era in which mathematical physics would go from strength to strength, and his works remain a source of wonder and admiration for those who have the patience to follow all the turnings of his mind, and to repeat his calculations. But Kepler also fascinates us by his psychological insight into the hopes and fears of his research, and by his joyous outcries when the goal has been reached and a new property of nature discovered. Recapitulating his work in the *Mysterium Cosmographicum* he wrote:

> And how intense my pleasure was at this discovery can never be explained in words. I no longer regretted the time wasted. Day and night I was consumed by computing in order to see whether this idea would agree with the Copernican orbits, or if my joy would be carried away by the wind.[63]

His excitement was caused by an idea that failed and was indeed carried away by the wind. No wonder that real success made him even more jubilant, as when he wrote about the discovery of the Third Law:

> Since the dawn 8 months ago, since the broad daylight 3 months ago, and since a few days ago when the Sun illuminated my wonderful speculations, nothing holds me back! I dare to confess frankly that I have stolen the Golden Vessels of the Egyptians to build a tabernacle for my God far from the bounds of Egypt . . . The die is cast, and I am writing the book, to be read now or by posterity, it matters not! It can wait a century for a reader, as God Himself has waited 6000 years for a witness.[64]

The reference to the Golden Vessels is significant. They were stolen by the people of Israel before the exodus from Egypt (cf. Exodus 12,35) as treasures not of their own making but acquired from a foreign world. This reminded Kepler of the way in which his most important discoveries were made. Every time he had tried to impress a mathematical structure of his own choice upon nature, he had failed. Success came unexpectedly and *a posteriori*. The discovery of the Third Law revealed that

> . . . the whole nature of harmonies in the celestial movements does really exist, but not in the way I previously thought, but in a completely different, yet absolutely perfect answer.[65]

His discoveries came as delightful surprises precisely because they were not the children of his own mind. Despite all the mental energy he had spent on unravelling them, they were, so to speak, stolen from a foreign country, or gifts from a foreign power.

It was Kepler's deep conviction that this "foreign" or extra-mental power was God. As he said in his very first work, the object of his study was

> . . . the Book of Nature which is so highly praised in the Holy Scriptures. Paul reminds the heathens that in it they can contemplate God like the Sun in water or a mirror.[66]

And in his last great exposition of astronomy the same idea is still, alive in his mind:

For it is precisely the universe which is that Book of Nature in
which God the Creator has revealed and depicted His essence and
what He wills with man, in a wordless [*alogos*] script.[67]

This conviction, that God reveals Himself in nature, leads Kepler to a particular
idea of the role of the natural scientist in which he found his juvenile aspirations
fulfilled. While working on his *Mysterium* he wrote to his former teacher
Maestlin that

I wished to be a theologian. For a long time I was troubled. But
look and see now how God shall be praised through my work.[68]

The possibility of praising God by scientific research did not fill him with pride,
but with stupefaction and fear. Realizing the immense seriousness of what he had
just written he continued:

But therefore I am so stupified that I must exclaim with Peter: Go
away from me for I am a sinful man![69]

And a couple of years later this new understanding of his role and vocation
caused him to use an expression which no one had dared to use before him:

Since we astronomers are Priests of the Most High God with
respect to the Book of Nature, it behooves us that we do not aim
at the glory of our own spirit, but above everything else at the
glory of God.[70]

Twenty years later he had found no reason to abandon this understanding. In a
dedication to the Emperor in 1618 Kepler explained that

I understand myself as a priest of God the Creator, appointed by
the liberality of Your Imperial Majesty.[71]

So this was what a scientist should be according to Kepler: a priest; not a priest
of nature for that would be the old paganism revived, but a priest of the Book of
Nature which he studies with awe and fear and great humility to the greater glory
of its author. A sinful man, yes, but nevertheless a man who had been given a
key to the mind of the Creator through the scientific insight into the secrets of
nature.

Here it is important to notice what kind of science it was that led Kepler to this understanding. As we have seen, Aristotle had denied that there was any wisdom to be found in mathematics, and by implication, in the mathematical discourse on nature; only the metaphysical understanding of the phenomena in terms of cause and effect would make it possible to discern their purpose and the existence of the First Cause of everything. But here Kepler was of another opinion: The student of nature can realize the glory of God even if he is unable to give a causal description of the internal
connections in the world. It is enough to discover that these connections exist. Kepler had himself discovered the laws of planetary motion without knowing the cause which produced them, and this very discovery had given his mind a special contact with the Creator of the universe. In the language of the three traditions, upon which I have so often relied in these lectures, this means that the context of Kepler's "priesthood" is the Archimedean tradition in which the causal account of nature is immaterial. This is not a far-fetched interpretation, for Kepler himself expressed it as clearly as one can wish. In the dedication of the *Astronomia Nova* he reminded his readers of King David who praised God in his Psalms for the wonders of the heavens, being

> . . . far removed from speculations about physical causes, being completely at rest with the greatness of God Who made all this.[72]

No more than David had Kepler been able to describe the heavens in terms of causality. Nevertheless, his mathematical astronomy had convinced him that the universe is possessed of a structure that is not impressed upon it, neither by the scientist nor by any other human being. The order of the universe is not a product of the human mind, but exists independently of it, waiting to be discovered. But it is important to notice that in the thought of Kepler this was much more that a belief in philosophical realism. His intellectual conquests did not lead to pride, but to humility by drawing the attention of the mind away from itself to that which is "given" from the outside.

The Two Books

With Kepler the metaphor of the Book of Nature came into its own as a vehicle of the self-understanding of a scientist who was deeply committed to the Christian faith. With Galileo the Book of Nature was confronted with the Book of Scripture, the Holy Bible itself, in a dramatic encounter which has ever since been regarded as one of the most decisive interactions between the world of science and the world of belief. For many it simply gave the final proof of the alleged incompatibility of these two worlds, testifying to an essential enmity between the Catholic Church, at least, and the scientific attitude. It is not possible here to go in any detail into all the intricacies of what has become known as the "Galileo Affair"; but we cannot avoid an attempt to delineate at least some of its essential features, in order to see whether this deplorable affair was a genuine interaction between faith and science, on a par with the previous encounters which we have already considered.

At the beginning we must remember that the scene of this affair is the first part of the 17th century when Europe was torn by deep and painful conflicts, many of which had originated in the Protestant Reformation one hundred years before. The Catholic Church tried eagerly to repair some of the abuses which had been criticized by the reformers. At the same time it tightened its theological reins, by a strict application of the decrees of the Council of Trent which had terminated only one year before the birth of Galileo. At the same time the Holy See became increasingly involved in the political tensions between Protestant and Catholic countries which finally exploded in the Thirty Years' War where, on purely religious criteria, it soon became impossible to distinguish friend from foe.

While these events shook the political and ecclesiastical world it became Galileo's fate to shake the scientific foundations of the inherited discourse on nature. In this he was not alone, but in the course of the events he came to occupy a more conspicuous position than that of the other great pioneers of the scientific reform. Copernicus had lived and worked almost unseen and unnoticed in a remote corner of Poland, and, even if Kepler was the official mathematician of the emperor, his works were too technical to attract the attention of more than a few experts on theoretical astronomy. But, after many years of quiet work at Pisa and Padua, Galileo suddenly rose to European fame in 1610 when he published the first results of his epoch-making observations with the new telescope he had constructed (but not invented).[73] All the world was amazed at the mountains on the moon, the many fixed stars invisible to the naked eye, the resolution of the Milky Way into individual stars, and the four satellites revolving around the planet Jupiter. The framework of the traditional cosmology had no room for such discoveries and would collapse under their weight, if they were not refuted; but this did not happen. On the contrary, Galileo's account of the heavens was verified by other scholars among whom were the Jesuits of the *Collegio Romano*, who had supported Galileo since his early years. Later followed the discovery of the sunspots, which were also observed independently by the German Jesuit, Christopher Scheiner, but the discovery was first published in 1613 by Galileo in a book in Italian in which he also publicly revealed his conviction that the Copernican system was true.[74]

At this time Galileo was back in his family city of Florence, employed as scientific adviser to the magnificent court of the Medicis, whose constant protection he enjoyed throughout all the vicissitudes of the rest of his life. Now it became clear that he had not only admirers, but also enemies who even formed a secret *Liga* for the purpose of discrediting him by fair means or foul. Among its known members were both churchmen and second rate academics; among the latter was Ludovico delle Colombe who had already published in 1611 a book in which he argued that the Copernican hypothesis of a moving earth was incompatible not only with Aristotelian cosmology, but also with the literal sense of several passages in the Bible in which the Earth is said to be at rest. He added that

> . . . all theologians without a single exception say that when Scripture can be understood according to the literal sense, it must never be interpreted in any other way.[75]

This indicated that the *Liga* had decided to wage the war against Galileo and the Copernicans in the theological field. The fact that the book was in Italian revealed that it was aimed at the general public outside the universities in an attempt to mobilize public opinion against its target.

At the beginning this and several other attacks on Galileo failed to produce any effect; but the efforts of the *Liga* culminated on the Fourth Sunday of Advent 1614 when a well known trouble maker, a young Dominican friar called Tommaso Caccini, preached a sermon in the Florentine Church of Santa Maria Novella in which he branded the idea of the motion of the earth as "close to heresy" and exposed the "mathematicians" as agents of the devil without, however, mentioning Galileo by name. Since in common parlance "mathematician" meant "astrologer", this was clearly a demagogic attempt to stir up the public, and the old and highly respected Florentine Dominican, Luigi Maraffi, felt obliged to write to Galileo to apologize for the conduct of his young confrère. But this was of no avail, for six weeks later the matter was delated to Rome, where the whole judicial machinery of the Holy Office was set in motion. The investigation lasted 13 months with several secret interrogations in Rome of people from near and far, who could testify to the opinions that were current among Galileo's pupils and friends. But nothing wrong was discovered and no personal accusations were made.

However, the Inquisitors was not the only ones busy in 1615. Down in Naples the Carmelite friar, Paolo Antonio Foscarini, argued in a printed pamphlet that the Copernican system was not incompatible with Holy Scripture. The aged Jesuit Cardinal, Robert Bellarmine, wrote to the author that

> If there were a real proof that the Sun is in the center of the universe . . . and does not go round the Earth, but the Earth round the Sun, then we would have to proceed with great circumspection in explaining passages of Scripture which seem to teach the contrary, and rather admit that we did not understand them than declare an opinion to be false which is proved to be true. But, as for myself, I shall not believe that there are such proofs until they are shown to me.[76]

This careful judgment did not pass unnoticed by Galileo who decided to answer both of the two questions that were clearly distinguished in the Cardinal's letter by providing proofs that: (1) there were scientific reasons for adopting the Copernican system; and (2) that it was compatible with the Bible.

With respect to the first question Galileo worked out a new theory of the tides, a phenomenon which had puzzled scientists since antiquity, in order to show that it could not be explained except on the assumption of the daily rotation of the Earth around its axis combined with its annual motion around the Sun.[77] The theory was certainly ingenious, but not completely satisfactory, and the opinion today is that it did not prove its point. However, Galileo went to Rome, to explain his "proof" to influential friends in high positions with the hope that he might be called as witness at the process, so that the Holy Office would not make any decision until the scientific side of the question was explained. But in this he was disappointed. The Inquisition never asked for his opinion, nor for that of any other competent scientist. Although hindsight is always deceptive, one cannot help wondering why Galileo did not offer the much stronger argument that could be framed on the basis of Kepler's first and second laws. These laws had been proved beyond any doubt in the *Astronomia Nova*, a copy of which was in Galileo's library. And even if they did not as such prove the Copernican system, it was clear that they made sense only in a Copernican framework. But Galileo missed this point.

The second question was dealt with by Galileo in a treatise formed as a *Letter to Madama Christina*. She was the dowager duchess of Florence, who knew Galileo well since he was one of the teachers of her son, and she had shown personal interest in the problem.[78] Galileo first explained how his enemies had wrongfully succeeded in bringing this matter before the Roman Court and he then went on to argue that purely astronomical theories cannot be matters of faith. In fact, all theologians agree that when the Bible speaks of God in anthropomorphic terms, its words are

> . . . set down in that manner in order to accommodate them to the
> capacities of the common people, rude and unlearned as they are,[79]

since such words are written for

> . . . the primary purpose of the salvation of souls and the service
> of God.[80]

The same principle must apply also when the Bible speaks of things that are not
divine since

> . . . the Holy Bible and the phenomena of nature proceed alike
> from the Divine Word, the former as the dictate of the Holy
> Spirit, and the latter as the executrix of God's commands.[81]

The two "books" have the same author and cannot contradict each other since

> . . . every truth is in agreement with all other truths, the truth of
> the Holy Writ cannot be contrary to the solid reasons and
> experiences of human knowledge.[82]

All this was carefully documented by Galileo with references to the Fathers of
the Church and more recent theologians, and was, of course, common Catholic
doctrine. But then the problem was how the Church could take action against the
new cosmology in spite of the "solid reasons" offered in its favor by the most
competent scientists? Here Galileo realized that this had something to do with an
unsatisfactory application of the decree on biblical exegesis promulgated by the
Council of Trent in 1546. Against private and arbitrary interpretations the
Council had ruled that no one is allowed

> . . . to twist the sense of Holy Scripture against the meaning
> which has been and is being held by our Holy Mother Church . .
> . [and in particular that one must not] interpret the Scripture
> contrary to the unanimous consensus of the Fathers.[83]

As a good Catholic Galileo did not question the authority of the Council; but he
denied that the instruction said that it was the *literal* sense of the Bible that must
be upheld whenever possible, as delle Colombe had maintained, and he had no
difficulty in supporting this view by references to St. Augustine and other Fathers
of the Church.

Furthermore, Galileo tried to clarify the notion of "consensus". A pronouncement of the Fathers can only be a matter of faith if the matters "have been actually discussed by the Fathers with great diligence, and debated *pro et contra*" until a common understanding had been reached. But, with respect to the motion of the Earth "it never so much as entered the thoughts of the Fathers to debate this question"[84] Consequently, they

> . . . cannot have decided anything about it, even in their own minds, and their disregard for it does not oblige us to accept a teaching which they never imposed even in intention.[85]

Therefore, since

> . . . this particular dispute does not occur among the ancient Fathers, it must be undertaken by the learned men of this present age.[86]

This was clearly an appeal to the Holy Office to consider the actual, scientific state of the matter before pronouncing judgment. But once again Galileo was disappointed. For, although his *Lettera* circulated in manuscript copies, we have no evidence that it was considered by, or even brought to the notice of, the tribunal. The Holy Office relied solely upon its own expertise and the advice of its *qualificatores* (a panel of eleven theologians none of whom were competent in astronomy) on two definite propositions to which the whole matter could be reduced.

The first proposition stated that

> The Sun is in the center of the world and completely immobile in space.[87]

On 24 February 1616, after only one week's deliberation, the *qualificatores* answered that

> All said that the said proposition is foolish and absurd in philosophy, and through and through heretical, since it clearly contradicts what Holy Scripture says in many places, both according to the strict sense of the words, and to the common exposition and the understanding [*sensus*] of the Holy Fathers and the Doctors of theology.

The second proposition was not about the Sun, but about the Earth of which it said that

> The Earth is neither in the center of the world nor immovable, but moving both as a whole and also with a daily motion.

On this the censure was that

> All said that this proposition must receive the same censure in philosophy and, with respect to theological truth, to be at least erroneous in faith.

The following day the Holy Office approved this decision and in March all the representatives of the Inquisition all over the world were informed of it. Copernicus's book was suspended "until it was corrected" and consequently placed on the *Index* together with Foscarini's pamphlet.

For Galileo's enemies in the *Liga* this was a most unsatisfactory outcome of their machinations. They had aimed at the downfall of Galileo. Instead they had obtained a condemnation of the Copernican system which did not even mention Galileo, who was able to return to Florence with a written declaration from Cardinal Bellarmine, who attested that no ecclesiastical steps had been taken against him. Of course, the *Liga* had to abide by the decision of the Holy Office; but the animosity against Galileo remained as a contributory cause of the proceedings taken against him in 1632 which had resulted in his condemnation and the abjuration of his Copernican conviction in the following year. This second judicial process is still full of unsolved historical problems, but, since it was more an attack on Galileo in person than a new theological evaluation of the Copernican system, we shall not here pursue this second act of the drama. We shall, rather, return briefly to the process of 1616.

The "Galileo Affair" raises the inevitable question as to how it was possible that the highest doctrinal office of the Church could make a decision which was wrong and truly fatal, since it contributed over the coming centuries to alienate people from the faith by exposing the Church as the enemy of scientific progress? What was it that went wrong? We must remember that in the 14th century radical innovators of cosmology like Thomas Bradwardine and Nicole Oresme had risen to high positions in the hierarchy, and that one hundred years later the even more revolutionary ideas of Nicolaus Cusanus had not prevented him from getting a Cardinal's hat. Although Copernicus himself had sometimes been regarded as a fool, he was never considered to be a heretic.

Why should everything be so different in the 17th century? In the course of time there have been many answers to this painful question.[88] Some have said that it was just typical of the Church to try to check the progress of science, although this claim simply disregards the historical evidence of the long period before Galileo. Other voices have deemed it wise of the Church to have wanted to protect her simple children from intellectual confusion, forgetting that this solution implies a cynical attitude toward truth. Still others underline that after all nobody knew at the time whether the Copernican system was true or false. This is correct, but it is not what the Holy Office said. It said that Copernicanism was false, and it did so without listening to the evidence which the other part was prepared to offer. Consequently, the "Galileo Affair" cannot be seen as a genuine meeting or interaction between Christian faith or theology and natural science, for science was not represented at the table.

Only one thing is certain: We cannot answer the question on the basis of preconceived ideas or prejudiced opinions. What is needed is a serious and thorough examination of all the evidence regarding not only Galileo, but also the cultural, political, scientific, and theological background of the ecclesiastical actions against his opinions and also against Galileo himself. It is good to know that no other than a former Archbishop of this city of Cracow, the present Pope John Paul II, has called for just such an investigation,[89] and that many scholars all over the world and of different religious affiliations are already engaged in this work. Of course, it is neither necessary nor desirable to "rehabilitate" Galileo, for history has abundantly vindicated his status both in science and in theology. Moreover, it is no longer possible to repair the damage which the "Galileo Affair" did to the Church by diminishing the credibility of its message and by compromising its image in the world of the educated. All we can hope for is that truth may prevail with respect to the "Galileo Affair" as it has prevailed long ago with respect to the Copernican system, and that the authorities of the Church will never again be tempted to make hasty judgments on insufficient evidence.

Notes

1.   1 Cor. 1, 23.

2.   1 Cor. 8, 4 ff.

3.   Acts 7, 2 ff.

4.   Acts 13, 15 ff.

5. Acts 17, 16 ff.

6. Job 38, 4.

7. Psalm 115, 1. See R.J. Clifford, "On the Old Testament Conception of Creation", in *Physics, Philosophy and Theology: A Common Quest for Understanding,* eds.: R.J. Russell, W.R. Stoeger, and G.V. Coyne (Notre Dame: University of Notre Dame Press, 1988) 151-170.

8. 1 John 4, 12.

9. Rom. 1, 19-20.

10. Cicero, *De natura deorum* I, 36.

11. John I, 1 ff.

12. Sextus Empiricus, *Adv. Math.* VII, 132.

13. See Diogenes Laertius, *Vitae Phil.* VII, 86 ff.

14. John 1, 14.

15. Augustine, *Confessiones* V, 3 and *De civitate Dei* V, 1-9.

16. Origen, *Contra Celsum* II, 60.

17. 1 Cor. 1, 20.

18. Phil. 4, 8.

19. Justinus, *Apol.* II, 13.

20. Origen, *De Principiis* IV, 2 and *Hom.II in Gen.*, Migne PG 12, 161.

21. See e.g. Origen, *Hom.III in Gen.* Migne PG 12, 176.

22. Augustine, *De Genesi ad litteram* I, 20, 39; Migne PL 34, 261.

23. Augustine, *Epist.* 82; Migne PL 33, 277; cf. *Contra Faustum* XI, 5; Migne PL 42, 249.

24. Augustine, *De Genesi ad litteram* IV, 7-8; Migne PL 34, 265.

25. Justinus, *Apol.* I, 59.

26. Clemens Alexandrinus, *Stromata* V, 14.

27. *Epist. ad Diognetus.* Chap. 7.

28. Origen, *De principiis* II, 1, 4 and I, 3, 3. The same idea was also expressed in the *Shepherd of Hermes* II, 1, 1. See St. Basil the Great, *Hom.II in Hexaem.* II, 5; Migne PG 29, 31-33.

29. Origen, *De Principiis* III, 5.

30. *Ibid.*

31. Aristotle, *Phys.* IV, 11; 219b.

32. Augustine, *De civitate Dei,* XX, 5.

33. Gregory Nazianzen, *Oratio* VIII, 7 ff.

34. Augustine, *Confessiones* XI, 11.

35. Augustine, *De civitate Dei* XII, 13.

36. *Isidore de Séville: Traité de la nature,* ed. J. Fontaine, (Bordeaux, 1960); see Migne PL 93, 963-1018.

37. *Isidori Hispalensis Episcopi Etymologiarum sive Originum libri XX,* ed. W.M. Lindsay (Oxford, 1911); see Migne PL 82, 73-128.

38. Isidore, *Etym.* III, 71 (no stars are seen together with the Sun).

39. *Ibid.* III, 27.

40.   *The Homilies of the Anglo-Saxon Church*, ed. and trans. by B. Thorpe,
      I-II (London, 1844-1846) *Sermon On the Beginning of Creation*, Thorpe
      I, 17.

41.   *Sermon on First Sunday in Lent*, Thorpe I, 173.

42.   *Sermon on the Epiphany*, Thorpe I, 111.

43.   *Sermon on the Circumcision*, Thorpe I, 103.

44.   A useful list of the principal translations is found in A.C. Crombie,
      Augustine to Galileo (London, 1952, and later editions) pp. 23-30.

45.   The most recent survey of Aristotelianism in the Middle Ages is L.
      Minio-Paluella, "Aristotle: Tradition and Influence", in *Dictionary of
      Scientific Biography*, Vol. I (New York, 1970) 267-281.

46.   See e.g. A.C. Crombie, *Robert Grosseteste and the Origins of
      Experimental Science 1100-1700* (Oxford, 1953).

47.   The text of these condemnations is published in Denifle and Chatelain,
      Chartularium Universitatis Parisiensis, Vol. I (Paris, 1889) 543 ff.

48.   For a brief survey of this problem see O. Pedersen, "The God of Space
      and Time", *Concilium* 166 (1983) 14.

49.   Augustine, *In Psalm.* 122, 4; Migne PL 34, 1632; cf. *De civitate Dei* XI,
      5.

50.   *Ibid.*

51.   *Questiones in Phys. Arist.* IV, q. 8, quoted from *A Source Book of
      Medieval Science*, ed. E. Grant (Cambridge, Massachusetts, 1974) 324.
      For the general debate on vacuum see E. Grant, *Much Ado About Nothing*
      (Cambridge, 1981).

52.   *De causa Dei*, Book I, Ch. 5; see *A Source Book of Medieval Science*, pp.
      556 ff.

53.   In his French *Le Livre du Ciel et du Monde*, a commentary on Aristotle's
       De caelo, ed. Menut and Denomy, in *Medieval Studies*, III-V (Toronto,
       1941-1943) .

54.   Nicolaus Cusanus, *De docta ignorantia*, Book I, Chap. 11-12.

55.   *De lineis, angulis et figuris*, in *Die philosophischen Werke des Robert
       Grosseteste, Bischofs von Lincoln*, ed. Baur (Münster i.W., 1912) 59.

56.   Roger Bacon, *Opus maius* II, 172 ff. ed. J.M. Bridges, (Oxford, 1897).

57.   Thomas Aquinas, *In lib. Boethii de Trinitate*, q. 5, a 3, ad 6^m.

58.   Edited by M. Clagett, *Osiris* 12 (1956) 73-175.

59.   See the many volumes of M. Clagett, *Archimedes in the Middle Ages*
       (Madison: 1964). See also his *Science of Mechanics in the Middle Ages*
       (Madison, 1959) and E.A. Moody and M. Clagett, *The Medieval Science
       of Weight* (Madison, 1952).

60.   For a further discussion of these topics see J.E. Murdoch, *"Mathesis in
       philosophiam scholasticam introducta*: The Rise and Development of
       Mathematics in 14th Century Philosophy and Theology", in *Arts Libéraux
       et Philosophie au Moyen Age* (Montreal-Paris, 1969) 215-256, and E.
       Grant and J.E. Murdoch, *Mathematics and its Applications to Science and
       Natural Philosophy in the Middle Ages* (Cambridge, 1987).

61.   See J.L.E. Dreyer, *Tycho Brahe*, p. 177.

62.   Autobiographical Essay from December 1597, in *Johannes Kepler:
       Selbstzeugnisse*, ed. F. Hammer (Stuttgart: 1971) p. 30. See *Opera Omnia*
       V (1864) 476-483.

63.   *Mysterium Cosmographicum*, Prefatio; *Gesammelte Werke* I (1938) p. 13.

64.   *Harmonices Mundi* V, Proemium; *Ges. Werke* VI (1940) 290.

65.   *Harmonices Mundi* V, Proemium; *Ges. Werke* VI (1940) 289.

66.   *Mysterium Cosmographicum*, Praefatio; *Ges. Werke* I (1938) 5.

67. *Epitome Astronomiae Copernicanae* (1618), *Ges. Werke* VII (1953) 25.

68. Letter to Maestlin 1595 October 3; *Ges. Werke* XIII (1953) 9.

69. *Ibid.*

70. Letter to Herwath von Hohenburg 1598 March 26; *Ges. Werke* XIII (1945) 193.

71. *Epit. Astr. Cop.* Dedic.; *Ges. Werke* VII (1953) 9.

72. *Astronomia Nova*, Dedic.; *Ges. Werke* III (1937) 31.

73. *Sidereus Nuncius* (Venice, 1610) in *Opere,* ed. A. Favaro, III, 51 ff. English translation in Stillman Drake, *Discoveries and Opinions of Galileo* (New York, 1957) 21-58.

74. *Istoria e Dimostrazioni intorno alle Macchie Solari* (Rome, 1613) in *Opere,* V, 71- 243.

75. L. delle Colombe, *Contro il moto della terra*, quoted from Galileo's *Opere,* III, 290.

76. Bellarmine's letter is printed in Galileo's *Opere,* XII, 159 ff. I have used a translation found in G. Santillana, *The Crime of Galileo* (Chicago, 1955) 98 ff.

77. Later Galileo included this theory in his *Dialogo* (1632) as the main subject of the discussion on the Fourth Day, see *Opere,* V, 377 ff.

78. *Lettera a Madama Christina*, in *Opere,* V, 309-348; English translation in Stillman Drake, *Discoveries and Opinions of Galileo* (New York, 1957) 175-216.

79. *Lettera, Opere,* V, 315.

80. *Ibid.,* 316.

81. *Ibid.*

82. *Ibid.,* 320.

83. *Conc. Trid. Sess. IV* (1546 April 8).

84. *Lettera, Opere,* V, 335.

85. *Ibid.*, 336.

86. *Ibid.*, 338.

87. The documents of the whole process were edited by A. Favaro in Galileo's *Opere,* XIX, 275 ff. A slightly more complete collection was published in 1984 by the Pontifical Academy of Sciences: *I Documenti del Processo di Galileo Galilei*, ed. Sergio M. Pagano (Vatican City State, 1984) pp. xxvii, 280.

88. See O. Pedersen, "Galileo and the Council of Trent (New Edition)", *Studi Galileiani* (Vatican City State, 1991).

89. See Pope John Paul II's allocution to the Pontifical Academy of Sciences on 10 November 1979, at the celebration of the centenary of Einstein's birth, in which he praised Galileo as one of the founders of modern physics and also a good Catholic with a sound understanding of the relations between science and theology. At the same time the Pope urged scholars to collaborate in a more profound investigation of the case of Galileo, "loyally admitting all wrongs done to him, no matter by whom".

III. THE IMPACT OF TIME

Old Traditions in a New Age

The time of Galileo has often been described as the great watershed in the history of science. Now the yoke of Aristotelianism was broken once and for all as the result of a brilliant succession of discoveries and new ideas. Similarly the persecution of Galileo and the condemnation of the Copernican system had discredited religious authority to the extent that it had lost all force in scientific matters. So at long last science had gotten rid of both the Philosopher and the Priest and was set free to enter the road towards a glorious future under its own steam and untrammelled by the power of irrational forces and authoritarian restraints.

This simple and hackneyed picture contains some truth and a fair amount of confusion. It is true that the great empirical conquests of the 17th century revealed many new and fascinating vistas. The telescope disclosed a universe of a vastly greater size and complexity than anyone had previously dreamed possible. Similarly, the microscope filled the world with minute details in both the organic and the inorganic domain with amazing consequences for anatomy and biology. The new continents across the ocean yielded a multitude of new species of plants and animals from different environments as material for a much more comprehensive natural history. And in theoretical fields there were new and admirable intellectual constructions attempting to reconstruct the universe on the basis of first principles enunciated in very different ways by Descartes and Newton.

On the other hand the picture of a totally new discourse on nature set off by a complete rejection of Aristotelianism was simplified to a degree which history is no longer able to accept. In fact, the alleged demise of the ideas of the Philosopher was a specious affair. Thus it gives food for thought to reflect upon the example of Galileo who spent all of his life demolishing one Aristotelian tenet in physics and cosmology after another. Nevertheless, towards the end of his life he explained to an old friend that he had already regarded himself as a good Aristotelian.[1] What he meant was that he had always recognized the Aristotelian principle of experience as the fountain-head of all scientific knowledge. This is true and is not contradicted by the fact that he often had found it useful to discard or suspend that causal description of the phenomena which to Aristotle was the all-pervading purpose of scientific investigation. For instance, Galileo was led to the discovery of the laws of free fall (one of the cornerstones of the new mechanics) by limiting himself

> . . . to investigate and demonstrate some of the properties of accelerated motion (in casu the fall) whatsoever the cause of this acceleration may be.[2]

In other words he postponed the question of gravity as the cause of the fall until the kinematics of the phenomenon had been precisely described. Clearly this procedure is non-Aristotelian and fits nicely into the Archimedean tradition which had, in fact, already in his early years deeply influenced Galileo. This was in harmony with Galileo's general views on the nature of scientific discourse as such. In a polemical passage directed against the view of one Lotario Sarsi (an alias for the Roman Jesuit Orazio Grassi) on the nature of comets he argued, in terms echoing the voice of Robert Grosseteste 400 years earlier, that

> Science is written in that Great Book which lies open to our eyes, -I mean the universe. But we cannot understand it unless we first know the language and learn the letters in which it is written. It is written in mathematical language, and its letters are triangles, circles, and other geometrical figures without which it is impossible to understand one single word of it.[3]

So for Galileo there was no total rejection of Aristotelianism. He upheld the principle of experience, but he abandoned the causal description at critical points of the investigations. Here Descartes took another view when he blamed Galileo for this methodological deviation, maintaining that it was futile to search for a law of nature

> . . . without having considered the first causes of nature . . . He [Galileo investigating free fall] has only looked for the reasons for certain particular effects and . . . thus he has built without a foundation.[4]

So here it was Descartes who came to the rescue of Aristotle, no doubt unconsciously, considering the repeated fulminations against the Philosopher which usually mark his works. Truly there were many mansions in the Aristotelian heaven where such different scientific attitudes could feel equally at home.

In this respect Newton occupied a position that had much in common with Galileo's attitude. It goes without saying that like everybody else Newton used the metaphysical discourse of cause and effect in his physical theories. It had become part and parcel of everyday language also in science. Nevertheless, at some of the decisive cross-roads of his scientific progress he found that he had to abandon it in order to overcome this or that obstacle to further developments. Also he was prepared to postpone the investigation of causes until the properties of their effects had been sufficiently explored. This clearly appeared in the discussions following the introduction of the hypothesis of universal gravitation in the *Principia* (1687). Since Newton had not proposed any "physical cause" of this universal force, he was attacked by Cartesian scientists for introducing an "occult" entity into the discourse on mechanics. What they meant was that they were unable to explain gravitational interaction in terms of collisions between elementary particles of matter. Newton replied, however, that

> . . . from the phenomena of nature we must learn which bodies attract each other, and according to which laws and in which ratios the attraction takes place, before we ask for the cause that produces it.[5]

Now to "learn from nature" about the mathematical relations inherent in phenomena was clearly an Archimedean approach. So we must admit that the Archimedean tradition was alive and playing a significant role in the foundation of classical mechanics.

Finally it is also possible to discern a Platonic voice in this chorus of competing methodologies. It can be heard in the rationalism of Descartes. It is true that the French philosopher was not a Platonist in the sense that he admitted a separate world of "ideas" as the real object of scientific knowledge. Nevertheless, he certainly believed that the properties of nature could be derived from "clear and indubitable concepts" which human reason was able to establish *a priori*.

These examples are sufficient to cast doubt upon the naive description of the "new science" as simply a victory over the Aristotelian tradition. For, while most of Aristotle's concrete doctrines in physics or cosmology were overthrown, essential elements of his philosophy survived unharmed, in particular the principle of experience. But at the same time the Archimedean tradition gave new and overwhelming proofs of its enigmatic, but indubitable fertility.

This leaves us with the other part of the picture. If science did not really get rid of the Philosopher, did it not finally get rid of the Priest? Or, otherwise expressed, did the age-long interaction between science and faith not come to a halt in the 17th century with a complete victory for science? And was this not a condition for the acquisition of more scientific insight into nature? Or, again, is it good history to maintain that, since the classical settlement crowned by the achievements of Newton, the scientific spirit has always militated against Christian faith? A complete answer to such questions would greatly surpass the narrow compass of a single lecture. Therefore, in what follows we shall only try to locate some of the historical prerequisites of a possible answer.

The God of Space and Time

Here it is interesting to realize the extent to which the very establishment of classical mechanics was influenced by theological thought. This has become clear over the last few decades through the growing knowledge of Newton's theological ideas. It has been known for a long time that Newton left a vast number of theological manuscripts. They were usually ignored by historians of science who were often inclined to regard them as aberrations of an ageing mind turning to "mysticism" after his scientific work was done. However, already in a manuscript *On Gravitation* from Newton's early years in Cambridge we find him wrestling with fundamental problems on the border between physics and theology. Among them was the old question of God and space which had occupied so many acute minds in the later Middle Ages, when the "imaginary" space "outside the world" appeared as what seemed to be a necessary condition for the belief in God's infinity and omnipresence. Now Newton realized that "if space is infinite, it will perhaps constitute God because of the perfection of infinity".[6] Behind this idea was perhaps Descartes's description of God as "a Nature which would have all the possible perfections I would be able to imagine".[7] Consequently, if one wished to avoid the heretical conclusion that infinite space is divine it was necessary to separate the idea of infinity from the idea of perfection. Here Newton argued very plainly that

> . . . an infinity of understanding, power, felicity, etc., is the supreme perfection; [but] an infinity of ignorance, impotence, misery, etc., is a supreme imperfection.[8]

With regard to space this separation implied that "an infinity of extension is [just] the perfection of being extended".[9] It is nothing more than that. In particular, it is not divine.

On the other hand, infinite space is to Newton something which, in common with God, is "of eternal duration and immutable nature".[10] So, if space is not a part of God's divine nature, then what is it? To answer this question Newton makes a clear break with the Aristotelian notion of space as related to the physical motion of a body. Instead Newton relates it to the metaphysical notion of "being", so that where Aristotle had said that, if there is a body, there is also a place, Newton is now able to say that: "No being (*ens*) exists or can exist which is not in some way related to space", with the result that "who posits being posits space".[11]

This metaphysical *volte-face* opens the door to Newton's new understanding of space which is purely theological:

> God is everywhere, a created mind is somewhere, and a body is in the space which it occupies, and that which is neither somewhere nor everywhere does not exist. It follows from this that space is an effect emanating from the primary existing Being (*spatium sit entis primario existentis effectus emanativus*).[12]

What this means is explained in what follows where Newton simply speaks of God instead of a "primary existing Being". The gist of the whole argument is that space exists because God exists, and for no other reason. This is *in nuce* all that Newton had to say about the ontology of space. Space is not a part of God's essential nature, but an effect or "emanation" of His ubiquity. It follows that Newton cannot speak of space as created, as the Fathers had done. Space is not contingent on the creative will of God, but it is more intimately connected with him in a way indicated by the rather obscure term "emanation", a word that reveals Newton's debt to Henry More and other Cambridge Platonists with whom he became acquainted as a student.

The public was only slowly allowed to share these ideas with their author; but in the first edition of the *Principia* (1687) Newton tried to translate them into a non-theological language, describing "absolute space" as something which

> . . . in its own nature, without relation to anything external, remains always similar and immovable,

contrary to "relative space" which is

> . . . some movable dimension or measure of the absolute space, which our senses determine by its position to bodies.[13]

Newton did not here explain the theological origin of the notion of absolute space. Therefore, it seemed to appear out of the blue as something that could not be derived from experience. Later positivistic philosophers of science have made this abundantly clear. However, Newton had not said his last word,

and in the Latin version of his *Opticks* (1706) he asked whether God must not
be conceived

> . . . as a being incorporeal, living, intelligent, omnipresent, Who
> in infinite space, as it were in His *sensorium*, sees the things
> themselves, and comprehends them wholly by their immediate
> presence to Himself.[14]

This tentative query led to a storm of discussion and protest. It seemed that space
was no longer a passive entity reflecting the being of God; it also played an
active role as the instrument of God's knowledge of the world. This meant that
God would know nothing if space did not exist. This is undoubtedly a radical
departure from the traditional notion of God as a transcendent Being who is
independent of anything external.

Among the thinkers who objected to this idea were both Berkeley and
Leibniz whose interventions in the discussion are well known. This part of the
story need not concern us here, and we must also disregard Newton's further
theological development towards an anti-Trinitarian attitude, whereby he rejected
the divine nature of Christ and placed Him in a subordinate position as the
"governor of the universe", at the same time as the Holy Spirit was reduced to
being simply the spirit of prophecy speaking through the Book of Daniel and the
Apocalypse.[15] This is of great importance for the history of Newton himself, as
well as for the understanding of how the neo-Arian and the Unitarian movements
developed in the 18th century. But these considerations seem to me to be
overshadowed by the fact that some of the principal tenets of classical physics
were worked out by Newton in a context that was theological through and
through.

The Confutation of Atheism

In the 17th century another note was also increasingly heard in the
intellectual concert in Europe. There was much talk about atheists and atheism.
This is somewhat mysterious. Previously Christian thought had paid very little
attention to atheism as such, although the Sceptics and Epicureans of antiquity
had always been remembered in short paragraphs in the history of philosophy.
But now there seems to have been a formidable scare of "atheism" rampant in
many circles. In Louvain the Jesuit, Leonard Lessius, published in 1613 a book

in which he maintained (without mentioning names) that there were many persons around who secretly "denied all Divine power and deity", being prevented by the law from disclosing their unbelief outside the narrow circles of their families.[16] Some years later the French Franciscan, Marin Mersenne, whose scientific correspondence with scholars all over Europe is well known, followed suit with another book in which he postulated the existence of no less than fifty thousand atheists in Paris alone (out of a total population of perhaps 400,000 inhabitants).[17]

This was clearly nonsense and can be explained only by Mersenne's all-embracing conception of an "atheist" as a person who did not subscribe to each and everyone of the elements of Catholic doctrine, or who was simply remiss in religious practice. In fact, real atheists were scarce. Among the philosophers there were very few who did not find a place for God in their various systems of thought, although sometimes in rather twisted ways. Even a thorough materialist like Thomas Hobbes denied that he was an atheist, since "god" played a significant role in his system of the world as described in the *Leviathan* (1651). But Hobbes's god was not only an impersonal "deity" which had set the world in motion without interfering in its later course; it was also a material being and part of the world itself. This explains why Henry More felt compelled to write against Hobbes in a book called *An Antidote Against Atheism* (1652).

All through the century the scare of atheism increased and believing scientists began to react to it. In 1690 there appeared *The Christian Virtuoso* by the pious Anglican scientist, Robert Boyle, who was worried about "the great and deplorable growth of irreligion", although he had a more sensible estimate of it than Mersenne, saying that

> I do not think there are so many speculative [i.e., theoretically convinced] atheists, as men are wont to imagine. And though my conversation has been pretty free and general among naturalists, yet I have met with so few true atheists.[18]

But this more realistic view did not prevent Boyle from leaving in his will the amount of fifty pounds for the endowment of a series of lectures to be given in London churches

> . . . to prove the truth of the Christian religion against infidels, without descending to any controversies among Christians, and to answer new difficulties, scruples, etc.[19]

So Boyle was also sufficiently scared to take positive action against the real or fictitious enemies of the Christian faith. We notice here the stipulation that the new lectures should avoid denominational controversies, atheism being regarded as the common enemy of all Christians, who ought to shelve their differences in order to present a united front against it. Here is an early example of that kind of ecumenism that stems more from fear of the world than from the fear of God.

Behind this new strategy against unbelief was the old distinction between the faith and the "prolegomena" of faith. Boyle nourished the orthodox belief that faith is granted to the soul by God as a gift of the Spirit; but it has philosophical prerequisites, such as the existence of God, which might be established by rational arguments if these were strong enough to convince rational minds without the assistance of grace. Consequently, philosophers were urged to prove that there was a rational basis for faith, and that it might be established not only by abstract reasoning, but might also be supported by scientific investigations.

Thus even before the middle of the century Descartes had presented the world with an apparently all-embracing scientific and philosophical synthesis as a substitute for the disqualified "Aristotelianism". In this system God occupied a very necessary position as the only security that the world really existed and that it was possible to know about its properties, in contrast to what idealists or scepticists might suppose. This explains why Descartes could say, with his own special form of modesty, that:

> I make bold as to say that never has faith been so strongly
> supported by human reasons, as it can be if my principles are
> followed.[20]

Newton also rallied to the defence. This was revealed when the young classical scholar Richard Bentley had delivered the first series of the new Boyle Lectures and was preparing their publication in a book with the significant title: *A Confutation of Atheism from the Origin and Frame of the World*.[21] The title shows that Bentley based his confutation on reasons borrowed from astronomy and cosmology, and it was understandable that, before the book went to the press, he asked Newton whether the new system of the world published in the *Principia* would provide arguments that would serve his purpose. Newton replied that

> When I wrote my treatise about our System, I had an Eye upon
> such Principles as might work with considering Men, for the
> belief of a Deity.[22]

This declaration is of some historical interest. It proves that Newton's theological speculations preceded the *Principia* instead of being a foible of his old age, and also that he had other than purely scientific motives for writing his great work, although they were well disguised in the text.

Newton was a mathematical physicist who had created a new theory of the universe on a large scale; but naturalists, concerned with nature on a smaller scale, also joined the ranks against the forces of irreligion. At almost the same time John Ray, the botanist and zoologist, published a book that was to become famous as a popular and easily understandable exposition of *The Wisdom of God Manifested in the Works of the Creation*,[23] as the highly programmatic title read. It dealt with

> The Heavenly Bodies, Elements, Meteors, Fossils, Vegetables, Animals (Beasts, Birds, Fishes, and Insects), more particularly . . . the Body of the Earth, its Figure, Motion, and Consistency, and in the admirable structure of the Bodies of Man, and other Animals; as also their Generation, etc., With Answers to some Objections,

to quote the long sub-title which shows that the author cast his net very widely, trying to mobilize all departments of nature for the battle.

Many other naturalists followed this pattern. There were the Boyle lecturers, Samuel Clarke[24] and William Derham[25], whose books were the first more or less systematic expositions of the ideas of "Natural Theology", a great movement which held a rather dominant position in Christian thought as a whole in the period of the Enlightenment.

The Theology of Nature

The "physico-theology" of the Enlightenment was one of the great movements in Christian thought and perhaps the last authentic interaction between science and theology. It certainly had an ecumenical character, being promoted by men belonging to both the Anglican, the Protestant, and the Catholic tradition, who were here able to ignore their mutual disagreements in favor of a common effort. For all their differences they had one feature in common: they all took science seriously. Some of them were notable scientists with original discoveries or theories to their credit. Others were keen observers of science, filled with enthusiasm for its progress, and confident that as Christian believers they had nothing to fear, but much to gain, every time a new page on the Book of Nature was opened for inspection. However, a closer look at the movement will show that it also was a rather complex fabric of different strands.

One such strand was largely concerned with the discourse on the universe as a whole. It derived mainly from the scientific success of Newton's *Principia*. This seminal work had not only put the science of mechanics on a sure footing, but had also provided a most impressive amount of new insight into such astronomical and geophysical phenomena as the motions of the earth and the planets around the sun , the orbits of the comets, the behavior of the tides, the precession of the equinoxes, and the figure of the earth. These and many other riddles of nature were now subjected to a mathematical description based on the same fundamental laws of motion, in connection with the assumption of a universal force of gravitation acting between any two bodies in the universe. It might seem as if Newton had pointed the way to an exhaustive reading of the Book of Nature in terms of mechanics; consequently, "mechanistic" philosophers gradually switched their allegiance from Descartes to Newton.

However, Newton himself was convinced that there were serious lacunae in the mechanical discourse on the universe. His own theory accounted very precisely for the motion of each planet in its elliptic orbit; but already in his first letter to Bentley he drew attention to a number of phenomena which theory was unable to explain, for instance, that all the planets move in orbits close to the plane of the ecliptic, that they all move in the same direction around the sun, and that their satellites also move in this way. Such remarkable agreements could not be inferred from the theory. Moreover, there was observational evidence that no undiscovered necessity would force the planets to move as they do, since we know that

> Comets descend into the Region of our Planets, and here move all
> manner of ways, going sometimes the same way with the planets,
> sometimes the contrary way, sometimes in cross ways, in Planes
> inclined to the Plane of the Ecliptic, and at all kinds of Angles.[26]

Now comets move according to the same general laws as the planets. It is, therefore, a fact that the theory does not prescribe any definite orbital plane for any body moving around the Sun. Tacitly assuming his theory to exhaust all the natural possibilities, Newton concluded that

. . . there is no natural cause which could determine all the Planets, both primary and secondary, to move the same way and in the same Plane, without any considerable variation.[27]

Consequently, these agreements "must have been the Effect of Counsel".[28] God must have willed it in this way.

Newton also presented Bentley with the further argument that the planets form what we today would call a "finely tuned" system, since their velocities are adjusted to their mean distances in such a way that their elliptical orbits are very nearly circular. The cause of this fact is unknown to theory. But

. . . to compare and adjust all these Things together, in so great a Variety of Bodies, argues that Cause to be not blind and fortuitous, but very well skilled in Mechanics and Geometry.[29]

It is almost as if God had read the *Principia*.

Finally there is an argument of a somewhat different kind since it concerns a possible consequence of the theory which has not yet been observed, namely, what is called by a modern expression the "gravitational collapse" of the universe. Gravitation is a universal attraction between bodies, and there is no evidence of a corresponding repulsion. "What hinders the fixed stars from falling upon one another"?[30] This question worried Newton almost all his life and it seems that he never arrived at a final opinion. In 1694 he told the astronomer David Gregory that

. . . a continued miracle is needed to prevent the Sun and the fixed Stars from rushing together through gravity.[31]

In 1713 he toyed with the idea that the final collapse could be avoided by assuming that the fixed stars are distributed in space in such a way that"their contrary attractions destroy their mutual actions".[32]   But this was a vague assumption which only shows that Newton wished to uphold the stability of the universe, just like the theologians who had always appealed to divine providence in order to prevent a universal destruction.

While Newton and his followers were busy with the great unsolved problems in cosmology and astronomy, the naturalists were more concerned with the "marvels of nature" in the biological world, as they appear to both ordinary and scientific observation. In both cases the basic idea was the same; but where the astronomers concentrated on strange phenomena that appeared as simple facts without any obvious purpose, the naturalists were struck by the testimonies to a design in nature. Thus the anatomy and optics of the eye moved Robert Boyle to exclaim that

> He that sees the admirable fabric of the coats, humors, and muscles of the eye, and how excellently all the parts are adapted to the making up of an organ of vision, can scarce forbear to believe that the author of nature intended it should serve the animal, to which it belongs, to see with.[33]

This was the old teleological argument, presented in a modern scientific dress. But it was not only single organs of the body which were adapted to their biological function. Living creatures were also adapted to the living conditions of their environments, as described by John Ray who listed numerous examples of "the exact Fitness of the Parts of the Bodies of Animals to every one's Nature and Manner of Living".[34] Thus the swine has a long snout so that it can dig in the ground without getting dirt in its eyes, and the camel has flat, broad and soft feet which are very fit to walking on the loose sand of the desert. He also describes with loving interest the marvels of the instinct of the bee, which builds hexagonal cells without waste of empty space or material, in order to store food as economically as possible; similarly there are insects which do not care for their young but, nevertheless, place their eggs where there is sufficient food for the larvae. All this sensible, and apparently rational, behavior would be impossible in animals "unless themselves were endowed with reason, or directed and acted upon by a superior intelligent cause".[35]

These were everyday observations; but other scholars were more impressed by the minute structures of life that were revealed by the microscope, such as the small organisms in a drop of water:

> . . . those minutest Animals have all the Joints, Bones, Muscles, Tendons and Nerves, necessary to that brisk and swift motion that many of them have; [this is] so stupendous a Piece of curious Art, as plainly manifesteth the Power and Wisdom of the infinite Contriver of those inimitable Fineries.[36]

From this observation of the mutually adapted minute details of a microscopic animal it is only a small step to the famous metaphor of the universe, not as a clock, but as a watch which led Bernard Nieuwentyt to ask:

> Would anyone think himself to be clever if, having found this watch in a lonely place, he firmly believed that it was not the

work of a skilled artisan who had assembled its parts, but that there were in the universe a non-intelligent law of nature which had collected and assembled its parts and joined so many pieces together.[37]

Here it is the mutual adaptation of the parts of the watch that impresses the author by the very complexity of the structure as a whole.

As time went on there was a shift of emphasis between these different strands of the great argument. In general, the organic world seemed to be a more useful basis than the doctrines of the heavens. This was recognized by William Paley who explained that

We deduce design from relation, aptitude and correspondence of parts. Some degree, therefore, of complexity is necessary to render a subject fit for this species of argument. But the heavenly bodies do not, except perhaps in the instance of Saturn's ring, present themselves to our observation as compounded of parts at all. This, which may be a perfection in them, is a disadvantage to us, as inquirers after their nature. They do not come within our mechanics. It follows that astronomy . . . is not the best medium through which to prove the agency of an intelligent creator.[38]

This clearly reflects the situation at Paley's time when astronomy, before the rise of astrophysics, had very little to tell about the individual celestial bodies. But Paley seems to overlook the fact that Newton's astronomical arguments were not concerned with a single planet, but with the planetary system as a whole in which there is no little complexity. Moreover, Paley's preference for the organic world had rather dangerous consequences. It contributed to narrowing the field of natural theology to the biological sciences, as if the phenomena of life were particularly fruitful as a testimony to the existence of a creator. This had consequences later when precisely these sciences came to the fore in the great debate about evolution.

A Dubious Achievement

Looking back upon this great movement one cannot but be impressed by the formidable outburst of intellectual energy among scientists and theologians who seriously wished to be able to underpin the old faith with the latest results of the new science. On the other hand one must also admit that the Natural Theology of the Enlightenment suffered from a number of shortcomings which were responsible not only for the downfall of the movement in the 19th century, but also for certain theological distortions that weakened the position of the faith when it came under serious attack from scientific quarters.

The fundamental theological idea was the often repeated words of St. Paul in Romans 1, 18-20, according to which it is possible to derive knowledge about the invisible God from His "works" in the visible world. As apostolic doctrine this was a safe point of departure to which no Christian believer would object. But the text did not make it explicit how such knowledge is actually obtained. This was left as a problem for future times. Natural Theology solved it in a particular manner which was, as we can see now, open to criticism both with respect to the implicit and fragile assumptions it made, and because of the much too restricted perspective in which it envisaged the task of theology.

Let us again consider Newton's contention that the common direction of the motion of the planets was a result of "design". The phenomenon itself was an indubitable fact. It was also correct that it was not a consequence of some natural necessity, since comets behaved differently under the influence of the same forces. So far, so good. But when Newton maintained that the common direction of motion could not be the result of chance, he had only purely intuitive reasons to offer. Daniel Bernoulli was the first to be able to calculate in 1732 the extremely small probability of this option.[39]   Furthermore, when Newton postulated that the phenomenon had no theoretical explanation he tacitly made two unwarranted assumptions. Firstly, that all the possible consequences of the gravitational theory of celestial mechanics had already been surveyed; but no one could say whether or not that was actually the case. In other words, one could not exclude the possibility that future theoretical developments might produce an explanation so that the theory could, as it were, repair its own defects. Secondly, Newton also assumed that there could be no alternative theory that would be able to explain this special phenomenon along with all the rest. He seems actually to have sincerely believed that his own theory had at long last provided the key to the physical universe as a whole. He had likewise thought that his work on the Biblical prophecies had provided the key to the riddles of human history.[40] All this meant that Newton's argument for the existence of a Deity rested on some rather dubious presuppositions, and that its eventual validity was a question of further scientific developments.

Considering the biological arguments for design used by the naturalists we arrive at a similar conclusion. Also here the point of departure was a series of solid facts. Nature does indeed provide numerous examples of how well adapted organs are to their function and how organisms are to their environments (and also some examples to the contrary), and to the apparently reasonable behavior of animals in their natural surroundings. Yet there was a significant difference between the two fields. The Newtonian astronomers had a general theory of mechanics which was believed to cover all large-scale physical phenomena. But the naturalists had no general biological theory that would enable them to say whether a phenomenon in the living world could be explained in natural terms or not. So also here the argument and its apologetic potential was left to the mercy of what the future had in store for the sciences of life.

However, the presuppositions of Natural Theology not only comprised scientifically established facts, but also a number of current ideas without any such foundation. Among them was a general belief in the stability of the world. The universe had come into being and might again disappear by divine intervention. But in between these events it would be preserved from essential changes by divine providence. In the organic world individuals would of course live and die; but it was generally assumed that their characteristic species would remain precisely as God had made them in the beginning. John Ray knew that there were strange fossils, indicating that "many species have been lost out of the world", but felt obliged to reject this idea which

> . . . both Philosophers and Divines are unwilling to admit, estimating the destruction of any one Species a dismembering of the Universe, and rendering the world imperfect. Whereas they think the Divine Providence is especially concerned and solicitous to secure and preserve the Works of the Creation.[41]

We have seen before how Newton toiled with the problem of the stability of the world at large, trying to find scientific reasons that would save it from gravitational collapse. But his anxiety was more general. Pointing to the internal friction between all moving parts of the universe he realized that since

> . . . the variety of Motion which we find in the world is always decreasing , there is a necessity of conserving and recruiting it by active Principles.

For if such principles did not operate

> . . . the Bodies of the Earth, Planets, Comets, Sun, and all things in them, would grow cold and freeze, and become inactive masses; and all Putrefaction, Generation, Vegetation and Life would cease, and the Planets and Comets would not remain in their Orbs.[42]

This was a remarkable foreboding of one of the great insights of 19th century thermodynamics. But Newton rejected this sad fate of the world and tried to find a guarantee "that Nature may be lasting".[43] To this purpose he hinted at a kind of atomic theory of matter which he never worked out in any detail. But the point is that he and his contemporaries took it for granted that the world would endure without real change, and that this was implied in the doctrine of Providence. Whether this doctrine really had this consequence was a theological question which was not discussed by the first champions of the movement.

Furthermore, when, for instance, Nieuwentyt argued that "the conservation and continuation of all things in the state and condition in which they were created in the beginning" was a proof of the existence of God, the argument was clearly becoming circular since the existence of God was in other connections used to explain the preservation of the world.[44]

However, there were more serious shortcomings of Natural Theology in the theological field, one of them being the intense concentration on proofs for the existence of God, as if this were the principal problem of Christian theology. Here there was a significant development. Robert Boyle still addressed himself to Christian believers, using scientific arguments to confirm them in the faith. But already Bentley directed his arguments against "Atheists, Deists, Pagans, Jews and Mahometans", forgetting that the two latter groups, at least, were already convinced of the existence of God.[45] And when Samuel Clarke delivered his version of the Boyle Lectures, he deliberately set out to present his argument in a style that resembled a mathematical exposition as far as the subject matter allowed, showing that only twelve propositions were necessary to obtain the desired proof.[46] This was no doubt an effort to accommodate an audience that had no faith, but that acknowledged the logic of a mathematical exposition. Nevertheless, this method had at least two serious consequences.

Firstly, the method was extremely dry. To let God appear as a logical consequence of a string of propositions might be satisfactory to minds imbued with the precepts of mathematical reason. It certainly seemed cold and dry to ordinary people who would always prefer a theology of the heart to a theology of the intellect. Viewed in this perspective, there is little doubt that the revivalist movements of Methodism in Britain and Pietism on the Continent were at least partly provoked by the meager spiritual diet offered by Natural Theology.

Secondly, the concentration on the existence of God tended to obscure the essential nature of the Christian faith. Both Jews and Muslims believed in one God; accordingly this belief was not the core of the Christian faith, but only one of its prolegomena. The Gospel was not a message that God existed, but a proclamation that God was incarnate in Christ Jesus who had come to save the world. In other words, the essential Christian mystery of the Holy Trinity was put on the back burner and the way opened towards both pure Deism and that 18th century chimera, the "natural religion" of all mankind, which saw the Christian revelation as a kind of non-rational and foreign super-structure, reducing Jesus to a mild and kind teacher of morality, one among many.

As we have seen above Newton himself provides a significant illustration of how the movement might lead to a diluted presentation of the central core of Christian faith, and it is easy to find other representatives of unitarian or deistic views among those who were influenced by the movement. But it goes without saying that there were others who realized the dangers and tried to extend the scope of Natural Theology in such a way that Christian revelation would not disappear from sight. This was the case of Samuel Clarke who first gave a course of lectures in which the existence of God was proved, but he continued with other courses on both natural religion and Christian revelation.[47] He was soon followed by Nieuwentyt who set himself two different tasks: firstly, to prove from the marvels of nature the existence of a "sage, powerful and clement Director of everything"; and, secondly, to prove that "the Bible, the Revealed word, stems from a supernatural and Divine Source".[48]

This attempt to integrate revealed truths into the discourse led to an inevitable change of method, for here the scientific presuppositions, the riddles and marvels of nature, were no longer of any use. In fact, Clarke did not base his second course on facts established by science, but on a theory of morality, and Nieuwentyt used an *argumentum ad hominem* to prove the truth of the Bible: it is regarded as divine by a multitude of men.[49] This is also true for the Koran, but, unlike the sacred book of the Muslims, the Bible contains predictions of future events which were unknown to its authors and could only stem from divine revelation. In both cases the arguments abandoned the scientific realm in favor of either ethical considerations, or historical investigations of prophecies fulfilled.

To conclude we must admit that for all its glory Natural Theology had its weaknesses and shortcomings from both a scientific, and from a philosophical and theological point of view. This explains its final disappearance from the scene, although this was a painful and protracted process. In 1829 Lord Bridgewater tried to keep it alive by endowing a series of monographs (directed by the Royal Society of London), written by renowned scientists and destined to promote very much the same purpose as the Boyle Lectures that had stopped long ago.[50] However, at this time this was a kind of artificial respiration which was unable to restore the vitality of a movement that had already lost much of its scientific support.

The Intrusion of Time

The inbred belief that nature must be stable and "lasting" had overshadowed the problem of time to which Christian thought had not given much attention since the time of the Fathers of the Church. When it once again came to the fore it was as a result of purely scientific investigations over two centuries, first in geology, mineralogy and comparative anatomy, and later also in theoretical physics. It all began when the anatomist, Niels Stensen (or Steno), in 1666 solved the riddle of fossils, showing them to be petrified remains of real animals or plants. Thus the *glossopetrae* from the mountains of Italy and Malta proved to be fossil teeth of sharks. This showed that at some time in the past these mountains must have been covered by the sea. A closer study of the landscape and fossils of Tuscany enabled Steno to distinguish six geological periods in two of which the region had been under water. This theory was supported by careful observations and argued with convincing reasons in Steno's *Prodromus* (1669), a seminal work containing the basic principles of both historical geology, crystallography, and paleontology which here emerged as new branches of natural history.[51]

Steno's pioneer work proved beyond any doubt that the face of the earth had not remained unchanged since the time of creation. Much more evidence for this assumption emerged during the 18th century, to a great extent in the form of fossils found in coal mines, but also in the form of surveys of the geological strata of the crust of the earth. These layers were often sharply separated from one another and contained fossil remains of extinct animals. Consequently, it was necessary to distinguish an increasing number of successive geological periods, separated by what looked like cataclysmic destructions of life. The last of these catastrophes was usually identified with the Deluge which was described as a historical fact in chapters 6 to 8 of Genesis. This interpretation provided geological support to the truth of the Biblical account.

However, the identification of more and more geological periods made it increasingly difficult to find room for them all within the less than 6000 years that had elapsed since the creation, according to the various, so-called "Biblical chronologies".[52] It was also difficult to imagine the nature of forces that could suddenly destroy the surface of the earth and as quickly restore it again to conditions fit for new forms of life. The debate on this problem began already in the 18th century to engage both scientists and theologians, and slowly the idea of a gradual development began to compete with the belief in universal catastrophes. Consequently, the belief that species could not become extinct began to crumble. Here there seem to be indications that the theologians began to take the lead. Thus Bishop Joseph Butler wrote in his famous *Analogy of Religion* (1758) that

> Men are impatient, and for precipitating things; but the Author of Nature appears deliberately throughout His operations, accomplishing His natural ends by slow successive steps.[53]

He was echoed by John Wesley who wrote in his own contribution to Natural Theology that

> From a plant to a man . . . the transition from one species to another is almost insensible. The polypus links the vegetable to the animal. The flying squirrel unites the bird to the quadruped. The ape bears affinity to the quadruped and to the man . . . The ape is a rough draft of man . . . There is a prodigious number of continued links between the most perfect man and the ape.[54]

No doubt this was rather amateurish zoology; but such ideas certainly helped to prepare the way for the more scientific treatments of the problem in the first part of the 19th century.

Here Georges Cuvier used all his competence in comparative anatomy to support both the belief in the fixity of species and the cataclysmic theory of the earth. However, on the very eve of the new century, Jean-Baptiste Lamarck denied that there were sharp border-lines between species, maintaining that more or less continuous transitions from one variety to another could take place under the influence of environmental changes, in conjunction with a more obscure "interior sentiment" in the living beings. Small changes of the individuals of a population might be inherited by later generations and finally result in differences on such a scale that it was reasonable to say that a new species had emerged. This theory of "gradualism" in the biological world was followed by a similar view in geology. In the 1820s Charles Lyell abandoned the idea of drastic cataclysms and special forces to produce them in an

> . . . attempt to explain the former changes of the earth's surface by reference to causes now in operation,[55]

to quote the sub-title of the famous work in which he gave a new direction to the whole science of geology. For the "causes now in operation" can be studied by direct observation of the action of wind and water on the earth's surface. But the implications of this bold idea were far-reaching. For the slowness with which these forces operate today implies that the recorded changes of the crust of the earth must have taken place over an immensely long period of time, perhaps hundreds of millions of years, although a precise estimate was difficult to make. Only one thing was clear, a "gradualistic" geology made it impossible to limit the age of the earth to 6000 years. So what would become of the "Mosaic" account of the early history of the earth as recorded in Genesis?

Already before Lyell's work appeared there were theologians who cried out against the attempts to cast doubt upon the Biblical record that were implicit in all gradualistic theories. A characteristic outcry came from a naturalist (and Methodist minister), Joseph Townsend, who formulated what may be called the battle-cry of all later "fundamentalist" opponents of evolutionary theories:

> The science of geology becomes of infinite importance, when we consider it as connected with our immortal hopes. These depend on the truth of revelation, and the whole system of revealed religion is ultimately connected with the veracity of Moses. The divine legation of Christ and of the Jewish lawgiver must stand or fall together. If the Mosaic account of the creation and of the deluge is true, and consequently the promises recorded by him well founded, we may retain our hopes; but, should the former be given up as false, we must renounce the latter.[56]

To make a correct geological theory a condition for human salvation was indubitably a serious matter, and believing geologists had to meet Townsend's challenge. One such scientist was William Buckland who used his inaugural lecture to the first chair of geology in Oxford (1819) to sort out the relations between geology and religion, maintaining that geology did actually offer proofs that the Mosaic account of the deluge had a sound basis, at the same time as he admitted the existence of fossils that were much more than 6000 years old. The dilemma was solved by the hypothesis that Moses described only the time from the creation of man about 6000 years ago to the Deluge, but that the earth as such had been formed much earlier and populated with the animals which had left these fossil remains behind.[57]

Townsend's intervention was by no means the only expression of a growing anxiety that science and faith might go their separate ways. But the storm did not really break until Charles Darwin's *Evolution of Species* emerged in 1859. The fundamental tenets of this epoch-making work owed much to Lamarck from whom Darwin borrowed the idea that there are chance variations among the individual members of a given species. Consequently, some individuals must be stronger than others and more fit to meet the challenges of their environment. But, where Lamarck had assumed the existence of an "interior sentiment" as an active principle of development, Darwin simply pointed to the ordinary struggle of life as responsible for a purely natural selection that would lead to the "survival of the fittest". Supposing that chance variations are inherited by future generations, it seemed possible to explain that some species could become extinct and others emerge. On this principle all past, present, and future species might be viewed as branches on one great, common tree of life. Man was no exception and in his *Descent of Man* (1871) Darwin argued that all primates (apes and man) were developed from a common ancestor species. This slow evolution of the organic world seemed to be unidirectional and to point, in spite of all decadence and decay, towards more and more complex forms of life.

The Darwinian "theory of evolution" caused a greater stir than any previous scientific theory had ever done. Many scientist tried to pick holes in it with different degrees of success. Others hailed it with enthusiasm as the final key to the mystery of life. But among both the lay and the learned it caused a public uproar as an impious denial of some of the most cherished opinions that seemed to be implied in the Christian faith. Like Lyell's geological theory it required a very long time scale for the history of life, and especially for the history of the human species. This militated against the "Biblical" chronology which was still widely accepted. The theory also admitted both the extinction of old species and the emergence of new ones, an apparent contradiction to the words of Scripture that on the Fifth Day God had created all plants and animals "according to their species" (Genesis 1, 24-25). Even more offensive was the idea that man had emerged at the end of a long chain of less developed species, and had not suddenly appeared by a special act of God as described in Genesis 2. But the worst blow of all was perhaps the idea that the biological evolution was kept going by variations caused by chance. It was generally believed that this was a denial of the doctrine of divine providence. It certainly knocked the bottom out of the argument from design which had been the apologetic mainstay of Natural Theology. Darwin himself was always reticent on disclosing his own views on such matters. But his son saw very clearly that

> We can no longer argue that, for instance, the beautiful hinge of
> a bivalve must have been made by an intelligent being, like the
> hinge of a door by man. There seems to be no more design in the
> variability of organic beings, and in the action of natural selection,
> than in the course which the wind blows.[58]

Thus the theory of evolution offered ample opportunities for a new and more profound examination of both the principles of Christian apologetics and of the dogmatic understanding of what the Christian faith really had to say about the origins of life. Unfortunately the debate was derailed at the very beginning when the Darwinian theory came up for discussion in 1860 at the Oxford meeting of the British Society for the Advancement of Science. Here the local Anglican bishop, Samuel Wilberforce, spoke (as the scientist he also was) about some of the difficulties of the theory, such as the problem of how the variations of individuals would accumulate in their progeny. Not unexpectedly he continued by stating his belief that the God of Nature is the same as the God of Revelation. However, at the end he made the fatal mistake of imputing to Darwinism the idea (which Darwin never held) that man as now existing is descended from apes. This gave rise to the mistaken impression that when the bishop criticized Darwinism in the name of science he was really attacking science in the name of religion.

This blunder was a godsend to enemies of dogmatic faith or even of religion in general who could now expose believers as scientific ignorants, a tune that was played in various modes by the biologist Ernst Haeckel in Germany[59] and in the United States by the positivist chemist, John William Draper,[60] and the historian, Andrew Dickson White,[61] while the British physicist John Tyndall[62] used a later meeting of the British Association (in Belfast 1874) to speak of religion as "our broken foe" which has no longer any claim to be heard in scientific matters. This led to an accusation against Tyndall of blasphemy, and to a pastoral letter from the Irish Catholic bishops condemning the idea of his Belfast address.

Brought down to this level the debate degenerated into what looks,in a historical perspective, like a crossfire of slang between two hostile camps. Militant anti-religious propagandists (some but not all were scientists) exposed the ignorance and obscurantism of theologians and churchmen who often responded by irresponsible talk about "science" as harmful to religion. However, a level-headed biologist like Thomas Henry Huxley stayed out of the fray, coining the word "agnostic" for his own attitude, while a few theologians also tried to estimate the situation on the basis of more considered and less partisan principles. Two examples must here suffice to illustrate this more balanced approach.

In 1884 the Anglican bishop, Frederick Temple, published his Bampton Lectures in which he gave a dignified and moderate reply to the shrill and aggressive Belfast speech of Tyndall ten years earlier. In the first part of these lectures he defended religion as a general human phenomenon, rooted in our spiritual nature and independent of experience, but, as a matter of fact, shaped in the form of Revelation. He continued by admitting that

. . . the enormous evidence in favor of the evolution of plants and animals is enormously great and increasing daily.[63]

He accepted practically the whole of the *Evolution of Species*, although with the critical remark that the transfer of variations from an individual to its progeny was not sufficiently described by Darwin, a point in which many biologists agreed. But his main point was that life cannot possibly be derived from inert matter. There was a time when the earth was too hot to make life possible. Later it became ready for it, "and life came, and no law of inert matter can account for its coming".[64] With respect to the Biblical account of the creation, Temple took a "liberal" view, maintaining that

> even those who contend for the literal interpretation of this part of the Bible will generally admit that the purpose of the Revelation is not to teach science. The author of Genesis had clearly no intention to say by what processes this creation was effected, or how long time it took . . . He saw the earth peopled, as we may say, by many varieties of plants and animals. He asserted that God made them all.[65]

Nevertheless, the Biblical author (he is no longer called Moses) had great ideas to communicate, such as the creation of all things out of nothing, and the not sudden, but successive, appearance of the various parts of nature,

> . . .and nothing, certainly, could more exactly match the doctrine of evolution than this. It is, in fact, the same thing said from a different point of view.[66]

Having explained this to the "evolutionists" he then reminded the "fundamentalists" (to use a modern term) that

> There is no more reason for setting aside Geology, because it does not agree in detail with Genesis, than there is for setting aside Astronomy because all through the Old Testament the sun is spoken of as going round the earth.[67]

This attempt to solve the conflict implied a complete separation of "science" and "religion". The old program of Natural Theology which based apologetics on the analogy between God and Nature is abandoned, and the grounds for belief are now found in some particular property of human nature, in which both faith and morality are at home without external support. This was less a solution than a removal of the problem. In practice it amounted to a complete separation of the two domains.

There was at least one Catholic theologian who took a carefully considered stand. Although it was not expressed in public, it is of some interest as a testimony to the diversity of opinions that were actually present in the Church. As a young student John Henry Newman had been much impressed by Buckland's geological lectures at Oxford, which helped him to form the opinion which he expressed some years later, when he wrote that

> . . . whatever I held then deliberately, I believe I hold now . . . as the abolition of the Jewish sabbath . . . , the Genius of the Gospel as a Law of Liberty . . . and the impropriety of forming Geological theories from Scripture.[68]

Much later he wrote to his friend Pusey on the occasion of Darwin's refusal to accept an honorary degree at Oxford

> . . . that that principle of propagation, which we are accustomed to believe began with Adam, . . . began in some common ancestor millions of years before. 1: Is this against the distinct teaching of the inspired text? If it is, then he advocates an anti-Christian theory. For myself, speaking under correction, I don't see that it does - contradict it. 2: Is it against Theism (putting Revelation aside)? I don't see how it can be. Else, the fact of a propagation from Adam is against Theism. If second causes are conceivable at all, an Almighty Agent being supposed, I don't see why the series should not last for millions of years as well as for thousands . . . Does Scripture contradict the theory? Was Adam not immediately taken from the dust of the earth? "All are of dust" - eccles. iii, 20 - yet we never were dust - we are from Fathers, why may not the same be the case with Adam? I don't say it is so - but, if the Sun does not go round the Earth and the earth stand still, as Scripture seems to say, I don't know why Adam needs be immediately out of dust . . . i.e. out of what really was dust and mud in its nature, before He made it what it was, living . . . Darwin does not profess to oppose Religion. I think he deserves a degree as much as many others who have one.[69]

Similarly he wrote to another friend:

I see nothing in the theory of evolution inconsistent with a
Almighty Creator and Protector.[70]

This open attitude led Newman to support the young Catholic biologist, St.
George Jackson Mivart, who had defended the facts of evolution (but criticized
Darwin) in a book which was savagely slaughtered in the Catholic Dublin
Review. This made Newman write to Mivart that there ought to be freedom in
the Church also for the supporters of evolution, but

> No one but will incur the jealous narrowness of those, who think
> no latitude of opinion, reasoning or thought is allowable in
> theological questions. Those who would not allow Galileo to
> reason 300 years ago will not allow any one else now. The past
> is no lesson for them for the present and the future; and their
> notion of stability in faith is ever to be repeating errors and then
> repeating retractations of them.[71]

However, Newman's protection did not reach beyond the grave and Mivart was
excommunicated by Cardinal Vaughan in the very year in which he died (1900),
a frightful reminder that even 40 years after Darwin the theory of evolution was
still a dangerous territory for Catholic scientists to enter. The role it came to play
shortly afterwards in the Roman campaign against "Modernism" further increased
the fear that the Church was about to stage another "Galileo Affair", as Newman
had intimated.

In fact, there were some similarities between the two cases. No more than
in 1616 did the Holy Office solicit the opinions of competent Catholic scholars
around the world, and now as then the battle was fought in the field of Biblical
exegesis. However, unlike the Copernican system, the theory of evolution was
never brought before a Roman court of incompetent judges. Instead Pope Leo
XIII established the Pontifical Biblical Commission (1902) which was later
supplemented by a research institution called the Pontifical Biblical Institute
(1909). When at last it was declared that the first eleven chapters of Genesis
were not historical in the ordinary sense of the word, the Scriptural objections to
the theory of evolution were officially removed.[72]

The debate on "science and religion" provoked by the theory of evolution
had many secondary issues which often obscured its essential features. These
appear more clearly now than a hundred years ago. Firstly, the apparently clear
division between "evolutionists" and "creationists" obscured the fact that both
parties had a wrong concept of "creation". In both camps this was taken to mean
that the world had emerged more or less in the way described in Genesis. The

evolutionists had no difficulty in demonstrating that the literal understanding of this text was incompatible with the scientific evidence. But, by understanding "creation" in the same way, their opponents forgot that the Christian dogma of creation is the assertion of a mystery which ordinary human language can circumscribe only in negative terms. Essentially it is (as mentioned in the first of these lectures) a denial that the world is constituted by anything within its own domain, man included. Emptied of this mystery and reduced to a pseudo-scientific myth based on Genesis, the belief in creation was drained of its force and had no charge against "evolution". Hence the jubilation on the one side and the despair and rage on the other.

Secondly, many of the theological attempts to come to terms with "evolution" led to unsatisfactory solutions and dangerous compromises. Frederick Temple was not alone in his attempt to place a "No Entry" sign for "science" in front of some inner sanctum of the mind. But his contention that science would never be able to explain the origin of life was a simple postulate. It may or may not be the case; but, in fact, it was only a new variation on a theme which the old Natural Theology had already exhausted. A particular domain of nature was singled out as so marvelous that it defied scientific inspection and, therefore, called for a divine explanation. This was dangerous because the argument would collapse if there came a time when a scientific discovery solved the riddle of how life appears out of inorganic matter. But it was also theologically unsound to speak in this way of the "God of Life", forgetting that God is the God of all creation and as necessary for the existence of a stone as of an animal.

Thirdly, the battle revealed that contemporary theology had also forgotten the essential role of time in the Christian discourse on the world. Christian thought had embraced the idea of a static universe whose features had been established in the beginning and would remain until the end, divine Providence being made responsible for the stability of both animal species and systems of stars. Changes were acknowledged in history, but not really in nature. This view ignored the much wider perspective in which St. Paul had viewed the matter, making room for the work of Christ on a universal scale. "The *whole* creation is groaning in labor until this day" (Rom 8, 22) for in Christ "God has made His peace with *everything* in heaven and on earth" (Col 1, 20). If this cosmic understanding of the history of salvation had been preserved, theology would have been better prepared for evolution and not shocked by the scientific demonstration that the mere passage of time is an essential factor in the discourse on nature. How inbred this static perspective was appears from the fact that it took a hundred years after Darwin before Teilhard de Chardin began to explore the theological implications of "evolution".

The conclusion of these hints must be that the debate on evolution was above all a testimony that all was not well in theology. Considered as an interaction between faith and science it was marked by the fact that faith was represented by a weak theology that largely ignored precisely those tenets of the faith that would have made a fruitful dialogue with evolutionary science possible.

Notes

1.   Galileo to Fortunio Liceti 1640 August 24, in *Opere,* XVIII, 234.

2.   Galileo, *Discorsi* (1638), Third Day, in *Opere,* VIII, 203.

3.   Galileo, *Il Saggiatore*, in *Opere*, VI, 232.

4.   Descartes in a letter to Mersenne 1638 October 11; cf. *Oeuvres de Descartes* II, 380.

5.   Newton, *Opticks*, Query 31 (added to Latin translation 1706) ed. E.T. Whittaker (London, 1931) 376.

6.   *De gravitatione*, published in A.R. Hall and M.B. Hall, *Unpublished Scientific Papers of Isaac Newton* (Cambridge, 1962) 102.

7.   Descartes, *Discours de la methode*, IVe Partie.

8.   Newton, *De Gravitatione*, 102 (see Note 6).

9.   *Ibid.,* 102.

10.   *Ibid.,* 104.

11.   *Ibid.,* 103.

12.   *Ibid.,* 103.

13.   Newton, *Principia*, Scholium to the definitions, Motte's translation, ed. F. Cajori (Berkeley, 1962) 5.

14.   *Opticks*, Query 28 (see Note 5) 370.

15.   See the editions of Newton's manuscripts in H. McLachlan, *Sir Isaac Newton: Theological Manuscripts* (Liverpool, 1950) and in F.E. Manuel, *The Religion of Isaac Newton* (Oxford, 1974); cf. F E. Manuel, *Isaac Newton Historian* (Cambridge, 1963).

16.   L. Lessius, *De providentia numinis et animi immortalitate* (Louvain, 1613) quoted from M. Buckley, "The Newtonian Settlement and the Origins of Atheism", in *Physics, Philosophy, and Theology: A Common Quest for Understanding,* eds. R.J. Russell, W.R. Stoeger, G.V. Coyne (Notre Dame: University of Notre Dame Press, 1988) 91.

17.   M. Mersenne, *L'impiété des Déistes, Athées, et Libertins de ce temps* (Paris, 1624) cf. Buckley, *op. cit.* (Note 16) 91.

18.   Robert Boyle, *The Christian Virtuoso* (London, 1690) 37.

19.   Quoted from J.P. Ferguson, *Dr. Samuel Clarke* (Kineton, 1976) 23.

20.   Descartes to Vatier, *Oeuvres de Descartes* I, 564.

21.   The book appeared in London in 1693.

22.   Newton, "First Letter to Bentley", p. 8, in *Four Letters from Sir Isaac Newton to Dr. Richard Bentley containing Arguments in Proof of a Deity* (London, 1756). There is a critical edition of the correspondence in *The Correspondence of Isaac Newton*, ed. H.W. Turnbull (Cambridge, 1961) III, 233-256.

23.   (London, 1691) and many later editions.

24.   Samuel Clarke, *A Discourse concerning the Being and Attributes of God* (London, 1705).

25.   William Derham, *Physico-Theology; or, a Demonstration of the Being and Attributes of God, from His Works of Creation* (London, 1713).

26.   "First Letter to Bentley" (see Note 22) 5.

27.   *Ibid.*

28.   *Ibid.*

29.   *Ibid.* 7.

30.   *Opticks*, Query 28 (see Note 5) 369.

31.   Quoted in *The Correspondence of Isaac Newton* (see Note 22) III, 334.

32.   *Principia*, 2nd ed. (1713) Prop. III, 14, Cor. 2.

33.   Robert Boyle, *A Disquisition about the final Causes of Natural Things* (London, 1688) 519.

34.   John Ray, *The Wisdom of God*, 139.

35.   *Ibid.*, 128.

36.   William Derham, *Physico-Theology* (see Note 25) 367.

37.   B. Nieuwentyt, *L'existence de Dieu démontrée par les merveilles de la nature* (1760); French translation of the Dutch edition (Amsterdam, 1716). This watch metaphor was later given a prominent place in chapter 1 of William Paley's *Natural Theology* (1802) and is often ascribed to him. Actually he quotes Nieuwentyt almost verbatim without mentioning his name, just as large parts of this famous book are only paraphrases from Ray's *Wisdom of God* and other similar works. See Charles Raven, *John Ray, Naturalist* (New Edition, 1986) 452.

38.   William Paley, *Natural Theology or, the Evidences of the Existence and Attributes of the Deity*, ed. B. Brougham (First Edition, London, 1802) XXII, 80.

39.   Published among the prize essays of the French Academy in *Recueil des pièces* 3 (1734) 95-144. D. Bernoulli emulated a calculation by John Arbuthnot who examined the preponderance of male over female births in London over a long span of years and found that the probability that it was due to chance was 2×10^{-82}; see *Philosophical Transactions* 27 (1710-12) 186-190.

40.   F.E. Manuel, *Isaac Newton Historian* (see Note 15).

41.   John Ray, *Three Physico-Theological Discourses* (London, 1693) 237.

42.   Newton, *Opticks*, Query 31 (see Note 5) 399 ff.

43.   *Ibid.*, 400.

44.   B. Nieuwentyt, *L'Existence de Dieu* (Amsterdam-Leipzig, 1760) 533.

45.   Bentley, in *Works*, ed. Dyce (1838) III, xv.

46.   Ferguson (see Note 19) 24 ff.

47.   The title of the collected edition of Clarke's Boyle Lectures was *A Discourse concerning the Being and Attributes of God, the Obligations of Natural Religion, and the Truth and Certainty of the Christian Revelation* (London, 1716).

48.   B. Nieuwentyt (see Note 44) Preface.

49.   *Ibid.* 29 ff.

50.   Lord Bridgewater (Francis Henry) left in his will 8000 Pounds for this purpose. The books should be

>   On the Power, Wisdom and Goodness of God as manifested in the Creation; illustrating such work by all reasonable arguments, as for instance the variety and formation of God's creatures in the animal, vegetable and mineral kingdoms; the effect of digestion and thereby of conversion; the construction of the hand of man and an infinite variety of other arguments; as also by discoveries ancient and modern, in arts, sciences and the whole extent of literature.

>   Quoted in C.E. Raven, *Natural Religion and Christian Theology*, (Cambridge, 1953) I, 210, where also the titles of the eight Bridgewater Treatises are listed.

51.   The *Prodromus* is published with other writings by Steno and provided with an English translation in G. Scherz, *Steno: Geological Papers* (*Acta Historica Scientiarum Naturalium et Medicinalium* Vol. 20: Odense, 1969). A facsimile edition of the *Prodromus* alone was published by E. Fabian (Berlin, 1988).

52.   R. Rappaport, *Geology and Orthodoxy: The Case of Noah's Flood in 18th Century Thought*, Brit. Journ. Hist. Science 11 (1978) 1.

53.   Joseph Butler, *The Analogy of Religion II,8*, ed. Gladstone (Oxford, 1896) I, 251.

54.   John Wesley, *A Survey of the Wisdom of God in Creation; or, a Compendium of Natural Philosophy* (Bristol, 1763).

55.   Charles Lyell, *Principles of Geology, I-III* (London, 1830-33).

56.   Joseph Townsend, *The Character of Moses Established for Veracity as an Historian, Recording Events from the Creation to the Deluge* (Bath, 1813) 430.

57.   The lecture was printed with the title: *Vindiciae Geologicae, or the Connection of Geology with Religion Explained* (Oxford, 1820). Buckland later developed his idea in a report on paleontological investigations in Scotland called *Reliquae Diluvianae* (London, 1823) and in his Bridgewater Treatise: *Geology and Mineralogy considered with Reference to Natural Theology, I-II* (London, 1836).

58.   Francis Darwin, *Life and Letters of Charles Darwin* (New York, 1888) I, 278 ff.

59.   E. Haeckel, *Natürliche Schöpfungs-Geschichte* (Berlin, 1868).

60.   J.W. Draper, *History of the Conflict Between Religion and Science* (New York, 1874).

61.   A.D. White, *History of the Warfare of Science with Theology in Christendom* (New York, 1896).

62   J. Tyndall, *Report to the British Association* (Belfast, 1874) 310.

63.   F. Temple, *The Relations between Religion and Science* (London, 1884) as quoted in T. Cosslett, *Science and Religion in the 19th Century* (Cambridge, 1984) 195.

64.   *Ibid.*, 196.

65.   *Ibid.*, 200.

66.   *Ibid.*, 201.

67.   *Ibid.*

68.   J.H. Newman in a letter to Whately 1834 November 11, in *Letters and Diaries IV* (Oxford, 1980) 358.

69.   Newman to Pusey 1870 June 5, *Letters and Diaries XXV*, 137 ff.

70.   Newman to Bishop David Brown 1874 April 4, *Letters and Diaries XXVII*, 43.

71.   Newman to Mivart 1876 May 28, *Letters and Diaries XXVII*, 71.

72.   In Pope Pius XII's Encyclical *Divino Afflante Spiritu* (1943) and the subsequent letter to Cardinal Suhard of Paris, *Acta Apostolicae Sedis* 40 (1948) 45-48.